Couples in Collusion

THE FAMILY THERAPY AND COUNSELING SERIES

Series Editor
Jon Carlson, Psy.D., Ed.D.

Kit S. Ng
Global Perspectives in Family Therapy: Development, Practice, Trends

Phyllis Erdman and Tom Caffery
Attachment and Family Systems: Conceptual, Empirical, and Therapeutic Relatedness

Wes Crenshaw
Treating Families and Children in the Child Protective System

Len Sperry
Assessment of Couples and Families: Contemporary and Cutting-Edge Strategies

Robert L. Smith and R. Esteban Montilla
Counseling and Family Therapy with Latino Populations: Strategies that Work

Catherine Ford Sori
Engaging Children in Family Therapy: Creative Approaches to Integrating Theory and Research in Clinical Practice

Paul R. Peluso
Infidelity: A Practitioner's Guide to Working with Couples in Crisis

Jill D. Onedera
The Role of Religion in Marriage and Family Counseling

Christine Kerr, Janice Hoshino, Judith Sutherland, Sharyl Parashak, and Linda McCarley
Family Art Therapy

Debra D. Castaldo
Divorced Without Children: Solution Focused Therapy With Women at Midlife

Phyllis Erdman and Kok-Mun Ng
Attachment: Expanding the Cultural Connections

Jon Carlson and Len Sperry
Recovering Intimacy in Love Relationships: A Clinician's Guide

Adam Zagelbaum and Jon Carlson
Working with Immigrant Families: A Practical Guide for Counselors

Shea M. Dunham, Shannon B. Dermer, and Jon Carlson
Poisonous Parenting: Toxic Relationships Between Parents and Their Adult Children

David K. Carson and Montserrat Casado-Kehoe
Case Studies in Couples Therapy: Theory-Based Approaches

Bret A. Moore
Handbook of Counseling Military Couples

Len Sperry
Family Assessment: Contemporary and Cutting-Edge Strategies, 2nd ed.

Patricia A. Robey, Robert E. Wubbolding, and Jon Carlson
Contemporary Issues in Couples Counseling: A Choice Theory and Reality Therapy Approach

Paul R. Peluso, Richard E. Watts, and Mindy Parsons
Changing Aging, Changing Family Therapy: Practicing With 21st-Century Realities

Dennis A. Bagarozzi
Couples in Collusion: Short-Term, Assessment-Based Strategies for Helping Couples Disarm Their Defenses

Couples in Collusion

Short-Term, Assessment-Based Strategies for Helping Couples Disarm Their Defenses

Dennis A. Bagarozzi

NEW YORK AND LONDON

This book is part of the Family Therapy and Counseling Series,
edited by Jon Carlson.

First published 2013
by Routledge
711 Third Avenue, New York, NY 10017

Simultaneously published in the UK
by Routledge
27 Church Road, Hove, East Sussex BN3 2FA

Routledge is an imprint of the Taylor & Francis Group, an informa business

Library of Congress Cataloging in Publication Data
Bagarozzi, Dennis A.
Couples in collusion : short-term, assessment-based strategies for helping couples disarm their defenses / Dennis A. Bagarozzi.
p. cm. — (Family therapy and counseling series)
Includes bibliographical references and index.
ISBN 978-0-415-80729-6 (hardcover : alk. paper) — ISBN 978-0-415-80730-2 (pbk. : alk. paper) 1. Marriage counseling. 2. Interpersonal relations. 3. Counseling psychology. I. Title.
RC488.5.B2695 2012
616.89'1562—dc23
2012005706

ISBN: 978-0-415-80729-6 (hbk)
ISBN: 978-0-415-80730-2 (pbk)
ISBN: 978-0-203-15234-8 (ebk)

Typeset in Berkeley
by Apex CoVantage

Printed and bound in the United States of America
by Edwards Brothers, Inc.

This book is dedicated to my grandchildren,
Trey, Nicholas, Dru, and Alex,
who make my heart smile.

Contents

Series Editor's Foreword

It seems a pity that psychology has destroyed all our knowledge of human nature.

—G. K. Chesterton, *London Observer*, December 9, 1934

Psychotherapy with couples is difficult and challenging, as the therapist needs to work with each individual's psychopathology as well as the interpersonal dynamics between them. In the professional training of marriage and family therapists this is discussed, but clear methods for truly understanding the deeper issues that keep a couple from a satisfying relationship are not provided. Dr. Bagarozzi provides a clear strategy for assessing a couple's problems that identifies the real dynamics that are keeping them stuck in a mutual collusion. Too much therapeutic effort today is placed on doing surface-level repair by focusing on presenting problems and ignoring these deeper processes.

Dr. Bagarozzi uses the term *collusion* to describe the various defense mechanisms that people who live in intimate relationships use to protect themselves and to maintain a comfortable relationship. To be effective, therapy needs to target these dysfunctional defense systems and replace them with rules that allow for mutual growth and development. It is unfortunate that even when therapy targets the collusion, it repairs the dysfunctional system and without creating a fully functioning one. This is done to satisfy the comfort level of both the couple and the therapist.

Couples in Collusion is a wonderful book that could only be written by a scholar and master therapist. Dr. Bagarozzi clearly describes the dynamics of couples in distress and explains how to assess and treat both partners and their roles in maintaining the disequilibrium. If you are truly interested in helping couples develop new levels of relationship happiness and satisfaction, this is your book. I want to thank Dr. Bagarozzi for this wonderful professional contribution to the Family Therapy and Counseling Series.

Jon Carlson, Psy.D., Ed.D.
Series Editor

Introduction

The term *collusion* describes a variety of defensive operations that people who live in intimate relationships use to validate and protect their respective selves and maintain dyadic equilibrium. These collusive systems are held in place by a number of unspoken contractual agreements and rules that exist at both conscious and unconscious levels of awareness. Professional assistance is often sought when these collusive arrangements have failed and the couple's attempts to reestablish its previously existing homeostatic balance have been unsuccessful. Fear that the therapist will require them to make changes in themselves and their relationship—changes that they are unprepared to make—often leads the couple to mobilize their characteristic collusive defenses during treatment. Paradoxically, it is the inadequacy of these very same defensive operations that is primarily responsible for the couple's difficulties.

Collusive defenses, like individual defenses, are universal. They are not necessarily pathological. Defenses and defensive systems are deemed to be dysfunctional only when they curtail the growth and development of the spouses or other family members or when the defensive operations interfere with the positive progression of a dyadic relationship or family system. For the most part, defenses used by couples who are seen in treatment are of this restrictive type. Helping couples develop a different rule system that does not require such confining and defensive operations is the desired therapeutic goal, but this may not be what the couple wish to achieve. A couple may consider treatment to be successfully completed once the previously existing homeostatic balance and collusive arrangements have been restored. The following example is illustrative:

A couple came in for treatment whose presenting problem was that the wife had become housebound. She had always feared being alone at night, but recently she had developed a variety of additional phobias that were accompanied by severe panic attacks. Over the years this couple's relationship had stabilized around the wife's phobias. Her fear of abandonment fueled the need for her husband to be physically, emotionally, and psychologically available to her in the evenings in order for her to feel secure, validated, and intimately connected with him (Bagarozzi, 2001). Being at home with his wife each night also allowed this introverted man to avoid attending work-related social events, which made him uncomfortable. The wife's condition began to deteriorate when her husband received a promotion that required him to work late one evening a week.

Contingency contracts were negotiated that required the husband to spend compensatory time with his wife on the weekend in exchange for his working late one night a week. As this contract became a routine part of the couple's relationship, the wife's phobic symptoms and panic attacks became less frequent and disappeared within a year's time. The couple then concluded therapy and were satisfied with the outcome. However, the wife still could not be left at home alone during the remaining evenings of the week. This ensured her husband's continued presence and also allowed him to opt out of most work-related social events. Essentially, the previously established homeostatic balance that had protected both spouses had been restored.

COLLUSIVE VALIDATION OF THE SELF AND SELF-ESTEEM

People who become intimately involved in a relationship such as marriage learn early on to identify those aspects of the other partner's self that are particularly vulnerable, require validation, and need protection. If an intimate relationship is to continue satisfactorily for any significant time, the partners must collusively agree to avoid doing or saying anything that would damage the defenses each has erected to protect these vital and vulnerable parts of the self. In my clinical work, I have seen couples who treat each other in ways that most people would consider offensive, punitive, degrading, disrespectful, and shocking, yet neither party chooses to leave the relationship, even though no barriers to termination exist and more rewarding alternatives appear to be available. In many cases, these couples stay together because the partners, in spite of the way they behave, have avoided attacking each other's vulnerabilities. They have not yet violated their mutually protective collusive agreements. The following example is a case in point.

Several years ago an exotic dancer and her husband came to see me for marital therapy. When asked to discuss their presenting problem, the wife said that her husband was "very inconsiderate." She went on to describe the most recent incident. One night, after she had finished dancing, she and her husband agreed to drive another dancer home. When they arrived at the woman's condominium, the husband offered to escort her to her door while his wife remained in their car. After waiting 30 minutes for her husband to return, she decided to see what might be keeping him for such a long time. Unannounced, she entered the woman's apartment and found her fellating her husband. I responded to this story with what I thought was an appropriately empathic statement. I said: "I can understand how you must have felt hurt, betrayed, and angry to find your husband having sex with another woman." The wife's response to my comment was quite surprising. She said: "I don't care that she was giving him a blow job. It was very inconsiderate and disrespectful for him to leave me in the car alone at three in the morning unprotected in a dangerous neighborhood for over half an hour. That's why I'm pissed!"

The unverbalized agreement that her husband would serve as her protector in exchange for her financially supporting him had been violated. Essentially, a line had been crossed. She then felt justified in attacking her husband's chief vulnerability—his inadequacy as a breadwinner and provider.

Support and validation of the partner's self and self-esteem are central to the collusive defensive process. The more fragile a person's self-esteem, the more sensitive his or her partner must be to ensuring its maintenance. Self-esteem has its genesis in one's family of origin during critical periods of personality development and becomes a more or less stable trait when one's identity has crystallized. Self-esteem is made up of two complexly interrelated components: personal worthiness and competence (Mruk, 1995). Worthiness is primarily affective. It is based upon how one feels about the self. Competence, on the other hand, is less subjective and has to do with one's appraisal and judgments concerning one's actual performance, capabilities, accomplishments, and so on. Being loved, cherished, and accepted as a separate and autonomous person by one's parents is central to the development of a sense of worthiness. It precedes the development of competence, since the estimation of one's competence requires the capacity for self-reflection. How closely worthiness and competence are linked in one's ideal self differs from individual to individual and can usually be traced to childhood family dynamics. Some children may feel loved and therefore worthy, irrespective of their competencies. In other cases, love, acceptance, and worthiness are conditional and contingent upon the child's accomplishments. Some time ago I treated a woman who was an accomplished pianist and recognized scholar in her profession. She suffered from low self-esteem and experienced periodic bouts of depression. Her father had been a decorated wing commander during the Second World War who desperately wanted a son to carry on his family's three-generation military tradition. This woman was the man's fourth daughter and represented his last attempt to have a son. Not only was she the "wrong gender," but she showed no interest in applying to the U.S. Air Force Academy.

Shortly after her father's death, this woman entered individual therapy for depression. The therapeutic process was a long and difficult one for her. As therapy progressed, she was able to forgive her father, and her self-esteem began to improve. She changed her eating habits, started exercising, lost 30 pounds, dressed more fashionably, and was able to accept herself as an attractive woman. For the first time in her life, she did not see being a woman as a handicap. Dating men, in the past, had often proven to be an unrewarding experience, since she tended to select men who validated her self-image as incompetent and undesirable. Learning to choose dating partners who appreciated her for herself and her talents led to her engagement to an older man who "treats me like a princess." It took her a while to accept that being treated like a princess "was not a bad thing."

During her courtship with her future husband, my patient disclosed how humiliated and insignificant she had sometimes felt in her father's presence, especially when his old wartime buddies came to visit. Although she had forgiven him, the damage to her self-esteem had not completely healed. The nonverbal collusive pact established between herself and her fiancé was that he would not bring up her painful childhood experiences, and she would never mention the fact that he had been incarcerated for selling marijuana when he was a college student.

In this volume, some suggestions for helping therapists identify a variety of restrictive and destructive collusive pacts that couples use to validate each other, bolster self-esteem, and maintain dyadic equilibrium are presented. Strategies that can be employed to help couples free themselves from such confining arrangements are then offered, along with a variety of case examples.

COLLUSION: AN OVERVIEW

The most common and easy to recognize forms of defensive collusion are those that have been termed "resistance." These include chronic lateness for appointments, missed or forgotten appointments, late cancellations, checks returned for insufficient funds, forgetting to pay one's bills, frequent requests for changes in appointment times, failure to remember or inability to complete agreed upon homework assignments and tasks, arriving for an appointment on the wrong day or at the wrong time, and so on. More often than not, one spouse is seen as resistant while the other appears to be motivated for treatment and to improve the relationship.

However, if the therapist focuses only on the behavior of the apparently resistant partner or sympathizes with the apparently motivated and cooperative spouse, the collusive nature of the resistance will go unnoticed and the therapist's attempts to help the couple to change will be in vain. The theoretical assumption here is that the spouses are locked in a power struggle. Neither will give up control of the relationship to the other. The partner who suggests that the couple enter therapy is setting new rules for the relationship, thereby controlling the other, who then attempts to counteract this maneuver through "passive-aggressive" strategies. Actually, neither partner is willing to allow the therapist to control *their* relationship by setting the rules for the couple, and a stalemate ensues. The behavior of the "resistant" partner can be seen as representing the couple's collusive defense.

In some instances, when standardized pretreatment assessment instruments are administered to help the therapist pinpoint salient problem areas in a couple's relationship, some couples may not be truthful in their responses in order to protect each other from unpleasant feelings (Bagarozzi, 2011). Sometimes, when personal histories are taken at the outset of therapy, spouses may deliberately collude to withhold vital information from the therapist in order to conceal significant issues such as substance abuse, domestic violence, illegal activities, or unusual sexual practices of which they are ashamed (Althof, 2007; Levine, 1988). As a result of such collusion, the true nature, scope, and depth of the couple's problems remain hidden from the therapist.

Symptomatic behavior in one spouse is another common collusive defense that couples use to protect each other, maintain dyadic stability, and resist change. Haley (1963) described how a claustrophobic woman's symptoms were used to maintain personal and marital equilibrium while protecting her husband by concealing the fact that he suffered from a fear of heights.

More-complex and less-obvious collusive arrangements have been discussed in detail by a number of writers. Some of these are reviewed below.

Dicks (1967) approaches couple collusion from an object relations theoretical perspective where transference, splitting, projection, introjection, and projective identification play major roles. For Dicks (1967), unconscious communication and collusion allow both partners an opportunity to fulfill unmet personal needs and rework unresolved conflicts through complementary role enactments, which serve to protect both spouses and stabilize their marriage. He identifies a number of collusive dynamics. These include the following:

Collusive Idealization: Central to the process of collusive idealization are reciprocal projection and introjection, where both spouses project good parental split objects onto each other while simultaneously denying and repressing their split off negative, bad, and destructive components. Both spouses then collude by introjecting these projections and behaving in ways that are consistent with these idealized projections. The result of this process is a jointly held defensive idealized marriage that validates and protects the spouses' selves. Treatment is sought when this contractual arrangement begins to unravel.

Negative Polarization: A similar process occurs when negative, bad, and destructive partial split objects are projected, introjected, and enacted by both spouses. Such marriages are often characterized by unresolvable conflicts, reciprocal negative exchanges, and arguments that sometimes culminate in violence. In such marriages, unresolved internal conflicts are externalized and played out collusively.

Collusive Projective Identification: In this process, parts of the self are projected and both spouses accommodate to these projections by introjecting them and then collusively playing out the required reciprocal roles. Once this projection-introjection process is complete, the spouses can treat each other in a variety of ways—for example, as one was actually treated or as one wished he or she had been treated by significant others during critical periods of development. Both good and bad selves are involved in this collusive projection-introjection enactment process.

Collusive idealization, negative polarization, and collusive projective identification are commonly found in relationships where both spouses have porous ego boundaries and poorly integrated selves.

Dysfunctional quid pro quo collusive contractual agreements devised by couples are the target of Sager's (1976) clinical approach. The contents of these contracts are influenced by each spouse's preconceived beliefs and expectations about the nature of marriage, personal needs, psychodynamic factors, biological forces, external influences, and values. An individual's contractual expectations exist at three levels of awareness:

1. Those that are consciously recognized, verbalized, and openly negotiated between the partners.
2. Those that are consciously recognized but not openly negotiated between the partners.
3. Those that are beyond awareness and unconsciously negotiated between the partners.

Treatment, for the most part, focuses on problematic unconscious collusive contractual clauses that have outlived their usefulness. Although these outmoded agreements may be distressing to both spouses, couples will often resist the therapist's effort to help them renegotiate more functional arrangements.

Psychoanalytically oriented clinicians were the first to describe how parents collude in the process of scapegoating a child in order to protect their fragile selves and avoid serious marital conflicts (Giffin, Johnson, & Litin, 1954; Johnson & Szurek, 1952). Vogel and Bell (1960) demonstrated how both parents colluded in using the defense of rationalization to justify their treatment of a scapegoated child.

Pioneering family therapists and clinical researchers have identified a variety of dysfunctional family structures and interaction patterns that evolve when parents collude in the scapegoating process. The majority of these collusive dynamics were observed in families having a schizophrenic child who served as the family's scapegoat. The most notable of these dynamics are reviewed below.

The Double Bind

In their classic paper *Toward a Theory of Schizophrenia,* Bateson, Jackson, Haley, and Weakland (1956) identified a unique type of communication pattern, termed the double bind, which characterized the family dynamics of schizophrenic patients. The major ingredients of a double binding family environment are as follows:

1. A family system that involves two or more members, most notably—a father, a mother, and the schizophrenic child. Since adjusting to a family system has survival value for the child, the child knows that he or she must accurately discriminate what sort of message or injunction is being communicated so that he or she can respond appropriately and thus avoid punishment.
2. The injunction or command issued to the child, however, is a paradoxical one, making compliance impossible.
3. The child is prohibited from metacommunicating about the absurd and contradictory nature of the message/injunction. Symptomatic behavior results when the child attempts to respond to these mutually exclusive injunctions.

In such families, the child serves as a buffer between estranged parents. The family dynamic usually takes the form where one parent, who is ambivalently overinvolved with the child, becomes primarily responsible for sending double-binding messages to the child. The other parent, in order to avoid open marital conflict, colludes by remaining aloof and doing nothing to protect the identified scapegoat.

Pseudomutuality

Wynne, Ryckoff, Day, and Hirsch (1958) have identified family systems where the parents' primary concern is the maintenance of what amounts to strict role complementarity between and among all members at the expense of the development of separate identities in the children. In pseudomutual family systems, any divergence from ascribed roles arouses intense anxiety in the parents. The rigidity of these fixed role arrangements allows the parents to avoid any hint of marital discord or difference, thus protecting them both and maintaining the family's equilibrium. Unlike families where the double bind is operative, both parents collude actively to maintain the pseudomutual façade.

Mystification

Lang (1965) used the term *mystification* to describe a process whereby a family member attempts to redefine another family member's feelings, perceptions, experiences, behaviors, realities, and so on in order to avoid open conflict or obscure the true nature of a conflict between them. For mystification to take place and continue for any significant period of time, the targeted person (child or spouse) must collude in the process by accepting the mystifier's definition of reality. Mystification is often seen in families that include a schizophrenic member. For some couples, mystification may come to resemble *a folie à deux*.

Invisible Loyalties and Collusion

Boszornemyi-Nagy and Spark (1973) focused on the intergenerational loyalty conflicts that prevent spouses from being fully committed to each other and developing a truly intimate relationship as husband and wife. Two spouses with strong loyalties to their families of origin may collude in telegraphing these loyalties to their respective families by having an openly conflicted and dissatisfying marriage. Boszormenyi-Nagy and Spark (1973) also described what they have termed a "collusively disloyal marriage," which presents itself as the polar opposite of these conflict-ridden and dissatisfying arrangements. "Collusively disloyal marriages" are formed when two people attempt to separate and individuate by totally rejecting or rebelling against their families of origin. The marital bond that these two individuals form actually represents a collusive defense that substitutes for true commitment and intimacy.

Myths, Collusion, and Cohesion

Ferreira (1963) first used the term *family myth* to describe a series of well-integrated beliefs collusively shared by all family members—myths that prescribe the static complementary role relationships that all family members are required to maintain in order to avoid conflict and ensure family homeostasis. Ferreira showed that these beliefs and roles could go unchallenged by family members in spite of the distortions of reality that were required to keep the myth intact. For Ferreira, the family myth represents the way the family appears to its members and not how the family may be seen by outsiders.

Anderson and Bagarozzi (1983, 1988) and Bagarozzi and Anderson (1982, 1988, 1989) extended the concept of family myths to include their morphogenic qualities. For these authors, family myths are seen as comprising a number of collusively shared beliefs, agreements, and contracts that are predominantly unconscious in nature. According to their theoretical formulations, family myths have three interrelated components. These include the following:

1. Each spouse's personal mythology, which is made up of a number of themes.
2. Conjugal/dyadic myths, which partners cocreate as the couple's relationship develops over time. These dyadic myths also incorporate the personal themes and myths of both spouses/partners.
3. Family group myths that evolve through the meshing, dovetailing, and integration of all the family members' (parents and children) personal mythologies, the conjugal myths of the spouses, parents' expectations for their children, and the shared experience of all family members.

Intervention focuses on the enhancement of growth-producing myths and the editing of those collusive myths and agreements that stand in the way of personal, dyadic, and family systems development.

Many of the collusive dynamics described above can be used by couples to resist change during therapy. These can be very subtle, as when the presenting problem itself serves as a collusive defense. On the other hand, blatant efforts to triangulate, provoke, mystify, and scapegoat the therapist are not uncommon. By using these tactics and others, both partners collude by claiming that they have made an honest attempt to improve their relationship but failed because the therapist was incompetent, unskilled, uncaring, prejudiced, or in some other way at fault.

It is important to keep in mind that collusion is a complex phenomenon. It can be used to validate the self and bolster self-esteem, avoid open conflict, stabilize the couple's relationship, and to defend the couple system when a threat is perceived. Although spouses may seek professional help for problems that exist in their marriage, they will often resist the therapist's attempts to help them negotiate more functional rules and contracts because doing so often requires substantial changes.

STUDY QUESTIONS

1. A couple enters treatment to resolve a specific conflict. This is the couple's stated goal, and the therapist agrees to help them work toward a mutually satisfying resolution. During the course of treatment, the therapist finds that the presenting problem actually represents a collusive defense that protects the couple from dealing with more serious relationship issues. If the couple succeeds in resolving the presenting conflict and is satisfied with the outcome of the treatment, what responsibility does the therapist have, if any, to bring these issues to the couple's attention? Explain your reasoning for the position you have taken.
2. If you believe that it is appropriate for the therapist to address the underlying issues with the couple, how should the therapist handle this situation, especially if he or she knows that long-term treatment would be required to treat the underlying issues and conflicts successfully?
3. Would it be considered self-serving on the therapist's part if he or she suggested that the couple consider continuing treatment long term in order to resolve these underlying issues and conflicts?
4. Could such a suggestion be considered unethical?

A Couple's Presentation as a Collusive Defense 1

In this chapter I offer some examples of how the presenting problem or problems for which couples seek treatment can serve as a collusive defense. The therapist is called upon to help them stop the downward destructive spiral and get back on track but not necessarily to overhaul their system entirely. Metaphorically, the couple is requesting a tune-up when a transmission service may be what is needed. Therapists, however, must consider that some transmissions can last for years, even though they are not serviced periodically. If the therapist is successful in helping couples regain their lost equilibrium, they will be more likely to return for help when the transmission begins to slip.

The presenting problem is used as a collusive defense when both partners have agreed beforehand what is to be discussed with the therapist and also, more important, what cannot be discussed. Even when empirically tested assessments are used to help couples and therapists pinpoint salient areas of concern and conflict, couples may choose to identify only those aspects of their relationship that are relatively safe, in the sense that these issues and concerns do not seriously threaten the integrities of the spouses' selves or the couple's equilibrium. The following case example illustrates this point.

BILL AND SUSAN

Bill and Susan had been married for 33 years when Susan contacted me for marital therapy. In the couple's initial interview, Susan enumerated a litany of complaints about her husband, while Bill sat silently. Her chief complaint was that she could no longer endure Bill's "passive-aggressive behavior." When I asked her to elaborate, Susan said that for the past few years Bill, a highly paid consultant and expert in his field, had been chronically late paying both state and federal taxes, leading to an accumulation of fines and penalties. Mortgage payments, credit card bills, and utility notices were often forgotten. Checks were routinely returned for insufficient funds because Bill had neglected to make timely deposits. He was usually late for appointments or forgot them entirely. The only area in which Bill remained responsible was in his professional life. He worked constantly and compulsively, but Susan suspected that sometimes, when he remained at his office late into the evening, he was doing so to avoid other commitments that he did not wish to honor. When Bill was asked to comment on Susan's characterizations of him and his behavior, he said that Susan did "nag" him periodically but that her criticisms were "mostly justified."

Couples who contract for marital therapy agree to participate in a six-session diagnostic and assessment process before formal treatment is begun. After the initial couple session, two separate individual interviews are scheduled for each spouse. During these sessions, personal histories are gathered, histories of all significant romantic relationships are taken, and each spouse's version of the couple's history is chronicled. These individual interviews are also used to formulate diagnoses and to speculate about possible collusive dynamics and defensive systems used by the couple. Each spouse is also asked to complete a battery of empirically tested instruments that have been developed to assess marital functioning, satisfaction, areas of conflict, and so on. When appropriate, additional assessments are used to address specific issues and problems not covered in the standard battery. When couples return for their final pretreatment session, they are given detailed feedback about the status of their relationship. Strengths and weaknesses are identified and discussed and treatment goals are agreed upon.

Bill arrived a half hour late for his first individual appointment and forgot to appear for his second scheduled visit, so that an additional session had to be arranged. He also failed to complete the assessment battery prior to the couple's feedback session, thus extending the assessment process for another week. Susan was exasperated by Bill's characteristic "irresponsible behavior" and spent the first 20 minutes of the feedback session scolding Bill and complaining to the therapist about her husband's behavior.

Attempts to involve the therapist in the couple's defensive system can take many forms. For example, the therapist might be seduced into siding with one spouse against the other, supporting the couple in attributing blame for their difficulties to external forces or individuals, scapegoating one or more of their children, and so on. In all such cases, the therapist's participation in this defensive process can be thought of as a countertransference to the system, which will stall therapeutic progress. In Bill and Susan's case, the therapist might be tempted to see Bill as the culprit and align with Susan against him, instead of seeing both spouses as cooperating in using Bill's behavior as a collusive defense that benefits them both.

Once the feedback session is concluded and assessment findings have been interpreted and discussed with the spouses, the couple is taught a hierarchically sequenced set of skills (e.g., communication, problem solving, and conflict negotiation) that they can use to resolve the problem areas in their relationship they have identified. Homework and practice to ensure the generalization of these critical skills are an essential part of the learning process. Inability to master these basic skills, repeated failure to complete homework assignments and practice exercises, and lack of follow-through with contracts agreed upon in sessions with the therapist are taken to mean that the couple feel threatened and thus have mobilized their collusive defenses.

Bill and Susan had identified finances and financial management as an important area of concern. Although they were able to learn the skills taught to them without any difficulty, neither spouse was able to make the agreed-upon changes needed to address the problem effectively. Susan avoided meeting with Bill to devise a budget, and Bill continued to bounce checks and forgot to make mortgage payments, etc. The couple then reactivated their defensive pattern. Susan nagged, Bill became contrite, but nothing changed.

Therapists who do not recognize the redundant and cyclical nature of this defensive process may become frustrated, since they tend to believe that they can do nothing to change it. Others may ask the couple to reconsider their commitment to change and suggest that the couple discontinue treatment until they are ready to fully participate in therapy. Strategic therapists, who have extensive experience dealing with resistance, can use a number of intervention strategies to break the cycle. For example, they might positively reframe Bill and Susan's resistance as a unique and creative way of staying intimately connected by engaging in periodic passionate conflict. They might predict noncompliance or failure to fulfill agreed upon contracts by relabeling them as understandable cautions before trying something new. Another strategy would be to use a restraining technique whereby Bill and Susan are cautioned against changing too quickly. Finally, the couple might be asked to use all the means at their disposal to avoid completing homework assignments so that they can learn to identify how they work together as a team to avoid doing tasks that they both consider to be unpleasant. This last strategic intervention comes very close to identifying the couple's behavior as a collusive defense, yet still avoids doing so.

Strategic interventions may be all that are necessary to help some couples move off dead-center, disrupt redundant cycles, and alter dysfunctional patterns without threatening the personal integrities of the spouses. However, sometimes they are not sufficient. When this is the case, the therapist should consider that the couple's defensive system is involved in protecting the spouses' fragile selves. Focusing on the issues that the couple has identified as problematic in the assessment process is a nonthreatening way to begin dealing with the couple's unspoken protective agreements.

In Bill and Susan's case, they were asked if assistance with devising a budget would be helpful. Both spouses agreed that it would. In the first budget planning session, it was disclosed that Susan had run up bills and credit card expenses totaling $20,000 in the last 6 months. For the past year, she had spent close to $35,000. Bill said, "Now, Dr. B., you see what I'm up against!" Susan was mildly apologetic and matter-of-factly said that she would have to curtail her spending. Over the years, the couple had developed an unspoken collusive agreement that would permit them to express negative emotions (e.g., sadness and anger) indirectly through financial channels, but recently the line had been crossed, the boundaries of homeostasis had been exceeded, and open conflict between them had broken out.

A Closer Look

Susan's parents were European immigrants who had come to the United States during the 1950s. Her father worked in the logging industry and her mother was a waitress. They could not afford to buy their own home, so the family lived in rented houses and apartments for most of Susan's young life. Susan described her father as a hardworking man and characterized her mother as an anxious woman who was always fearful that she and her husband would be unable to meet their expenses. Frequently, her mother would say that the family was "only an onion skin away from eviction." Her parents' financial concerns were all-consuming. They worked long hours to make ends meet and had little time for Susan and her younger sister. Early on, Susan vowed that she would not live as her parents did. She said that for most of her adolescence she felt "sad and empty."

After graduating from high school, Susan worked as a teller in her hometown bank until she had saved enough money to move to the city. Bill was attending graduate school when they met. He was tall, gaunt, and socially inept but a superior student. Susan was a striking woman who had never experienced any difficulty attracting men, and she used her good looks to her advantage. Bill was flattered when she showed interest in him. His friends urged him to ask Susan for a date, and he was shocked when she agreed to go out with him. They began to date steadily and married shortly after Bill received his MBA.

Bill's self-esteem was predominantly competence-based. In his family, worthiness was directly linked to his performance. Bill knew that his parents loved him, but he experienced their love as conditional. Bill suspected that Susan's attraction to him was also based to a large degree on his earning potential. Given the importance his parents placed on achievement, it was not surprising that they had some questions about why a woman as beautiful as Susan would want to marry an ordinary-looking, immature, inexperienced young man like Bill. Nevertheless, Susan proved to be a faithful wife and good mother. Bill chose not to discuss Susan's spending habits with his parents, so as not to reactivate their concerns, but his resentment grew even though he understood the reasons for her increased spending—her nonverbalized anger and her attempts to fill the emptiness that had become unbearable when their last child left home. Bill expressed his anger indirectly in ways that would strike at the heart of Susan's greatest fear and vulnerability. Late notices and penalties for missed mortgage payments would bring to mind Susan's mother's lament of being "only an onion skin away from eviction."

Mounting debt exceeded the homeostatic set point that the couple had established for dealing with negative feelings through financial channels. They then turned to attacking those vulnerabilities in each other that they had implicitly agreed to protect in the past. In response to Bill's complaint about Susan's spending, she attacked his adequacy as a provider—that is, his competence. Bill responded by suggesting that one way for the couple to get out of debt would be to sell their home and purchase a less expensive condominium—symbolically threatening eviction and her sense of security.

Bringing to the couple's awareness the mutually agreed upon rules for expressing anger indirectly through financial channels and the self-protective functions they might be serving moved the therapy in a very different direction. The development of mutual trust, respect, and self-validation became the immediate focus of treatment. Learning more functional and direct ways to express anger and disagreement followed, and Susan was able to curtail her spending to a degree that did not threaten the couple's equilibrium.

It is important to keep in mind that behavioral transactions between spouses and individuals involved in intimate relationships are often symbolic in nature.

Helping couples to negotiate exchange contracts that do not take into consideration each participant's symbol system may result in agreements that are short-lived (Bagarozzi, 1981).

Homeostasis having been restored, Bill and Susan concluded therapy. A 1-year follow-up revealed that the exchange agreements Susan and Bill had made in therapy had remained in place. Susan had curbed her spending considerably and Bill had been prompt in paying bills, filing taxes in a timely fashion, and bouncing fewer checks. Both agreed that the couple had come a long way in expressing anger more directly and dealing with conflicts more constructively. Susan said she had been considering entering individual therapy to deal with her "emptiness" and to resolve some issues having to do with her parents. I agreed to treat her when she felt she was ready. Bill was supportive of her decision.

CLARA AND FRED

This couple was referred for sex therapy by Clara's gynecologist after Clara mentioned to her, offhandedly, that the frequency of sexual relations with her husband had declined over the past 2 years. Her gynecologist thought it odd that Clara was only mildly distressed about this issue, since Clara and her husband had had an active and satisfying sex life for as long as the gynecologist had known her. The presenting problem was identified as decreased sexual activity.

Personal histories and sex histories for both Clara and Fred were unremarkable. Measures of marital satisfaction, areas of possible marital conflict, intimacy, and assessment of intergenerational dynamics did not reveal any significant problems or concerns. Clara was 36 years old and Fred had just celebrated his 43rd birthday. Since women and men reach their sexual peaks at different times in their lives, a woman's true level of desire for sexual intercourse, orgasm, and sexual intimacy may not emerge until she is in her late thirties or early forties. However, by the time many men reach the age of 40, their desire for sexual activity may have decreased considerably. Both Clara and Fred dismissed as improbable the possibility that a discrepancy in sexual desire might be contributing to a reduction in their sexual activity. They colluded in denying that such a difference might have developed between them.

For some couples, any acknowledgment of differences is threatening to dyadic stability and personal integrity. Such couples are usually involved in enmeshed relationships. Persons with defective ego boundaries and poorly integrated selves who have not successfully completed the process of separation-individuation are particularly prone to forming such relationships. Some time ago I treated a couple who had been married for 39 years. They began to date exclusively during their sophomore year in high school and married shortly after graduation. For this couple, the distinction between personal identity and dyadic identity had not been established. Their denial of any differences in critical areas of their relationship was reinforced by scriptural teachings mandating that a man should leave his father and his mother and "cleave to his wife," so that they become as "one flesh."

Although it would not be accurate to say that Clara and Fred were enmeshed to the point where individual ego boundaries were blurred and personal identities were unclear, they still could not entertain the possibility that a desire discrepancy had developed between them. Such an admission would reveal that Fred, indeed, had become less interested in sex, while Clara's need for sexual involvement had increased. Denying these differences protected their self-esteem, validated Fred's self-image, and allowed them to maintain the conjugal myth of a sexually vibrant couple.

Spouses' individual defense mechanisms often interact in a complementary fashion. For example, a wife may *deny* her abuse of prescription drugs while her husband *rationalizes* her use of them by saying that she "only uses them to help her sleep"; a wife aids in her husband's *repression* of traumatic childhood experiences by *avoiding* any topic that might call to mind these upsetting memories; or a husband may attribute his unacceptable personal qualities to a neighbor while his wife supports these *projections* by *devaluing* the man, and so on. Over the years these interlocking defensive patterns become characteristic of how couples deal with anxiety-producing and threatening experiences. It is helpful to keep in mind that the spouses' personal defenses are often linked in some complex fashion.

PROVOCATION AS A COLLUSIVE DEFENSE

Defensive strategies that are meant to provoke the therapist usually appear during the initial stages of treatment. For example, Bill's lateness for his first individual session, his failure to keep his second appointment, and his forgetting to complete the assessment battery are good examples of provocative behaviors. As mentioned earlier, a countertransferential response to such provocations will render the therapist ineffective. Such provocative behavior is easy to recognize. If the therapist does not respond countertransferentially, the spouses will be more likely to trust him or her with the vulnerable and protected aspects of themselves and their relationship.

Provocation to respond countertransferentially may not always take a negative form. Praise and flattery of the therapist can have the same effect if the therapist responds in a countertransferential manner. Trying to live up to a couple's idealizations and unrealistic expectations may prevent a therapist from behaving in ways that are therapeutically appropriate and in the couple's best interest. Several years ago a colleague of mine referred one of his doctoral students and his wife to me for marital therapy. The young man had read a number of articles and books that I had written. One of his first remarks to me was that he felt privileged that I had agreed to see him and his wife in therapy; moreover, he believed that "if anyone can fix our marriage, you can." It would be dishonest to say that I did not feel flattered, but I also felt that I was being set up. I thanked him for his kind words and then added that all I could do was to help the couple acquire the tools that would enable them to fix their own marriage. Some provocations take the form of direct challenges to the therapist. For example, when Peter and Cindy came in for their first appointment, Peter candidly stated that he did not want to be in therapy and that Cindy had "drug me in here to be therapized." He added that he did not see any point in paying someone to solve their problems, and that he and Cindy should be able to solve their own problems without anyone else's "interference." Peter then looked at me directly and said: "I'm not about to have some therapist try to change me. I'm perfectly happy the way I am."

The countertransferential pull here would be to try to convince Peter to accept the value of therapy. By doing this, however, the therapist would be perceived as aligning himself with Cindy, who had been a staunch advocate of counseling. In such cases, a direct, matter-of-fact, didactic approach can be used to dispel such a perception and eliminate any perceived threat to the self. If the therapist becomes defensive, however, he or she would be taking the bait and rendered ineffective. The following comments were addressed to the couple and not specifically to Peter:

> Before we begin, I would like to make a few remarks about marriage counseling. Marriage counseling is a skills-focused learning approach. Just the way some folks will hire a golf pro or a tennis instructor to help them improve their game, some people use the services of a counselor to help them acquire new skills that they can use to improve their marriage. The most common skills I teach couples include communication, conflict negotiation, problem solving, and goal setting. Learning to use these new skill sets outside of this office is important so there is homework involved. The quicker couples learn how to use these new skills to solve their problems, the shorter the counseling process.
>
> The goal of marriage counseling is to help couples change the way they treat each other. Behavior change is the focus and not personality change. Personality changes or changes in personality traits are very difficult to achieve, and such changes can only come about with a person's full cooperation. Such changes, if they do occur, take a long time.

> Since marriage counseling is focused on learning new skills, it is considered brief or short-term counseling.
>
> Do you have any questions?

The use of the term *marriage counseling* is deliberate. Doing so depathologizes the process and is less threatening to the self. Emphasizing the dimension of behavioral skills acquisition further reduces the threat. The belief that therapists possess secret skills, techniques, powers, and so on that they can use to change people against their will or without their knowledge is sometimes encountered at the outset of treatment. Reassurance that structural changes in the self/personality can come about only with the person's full cooperation tends to allay such anxiety. For many men, asking for help is painful and is often seen as admitting to certain inadequacies (i.e., incompetence). It has been my experience that some men are more likely to be receptive to therapy if a sports analogy is used to explain the process. Provocations, whether they are positive or negative, subtle or blatant, can be seen as the couple's attempt to influence how the therapist perceives each spouse and the couple's relationship at the outset of therapy.

It is important for the therapist to remember that provocation by one spouse still represents a couple's defense. When negative provocations are used, it might be helpful to think of the spouses as being engaged in a collusive "good cop/bad cop" strategy.

SCAPEGOATING THE THERAPIST

As mentioned earlier, scapegoating the therapist is another type of collusive defense that couples sometimes use to avoid entering treatment. The following examples are offered to illustrate this point.

1. As a psychological consultant to the Catholic Archdiocese of Atlanta, I have received a number of referrals from the clergy. On one occasion, a Catholic couple contacted me for marital therapy at the suggestion of their priest. About halfway through my first interview with them, the husband asked if my counseling was guided by Church teachings, specifically the *Catechism of the Catholic Church*. I responded by saying that I saw my role as helping the couple acquire skills that would enable them to resolve the conflicts that had brought them in to see me. I added that questions about faith, morals, and Catholic teachings were best answered by Father Thomas, the priest who

had referred them to me. The wife then asked if I believed in divorce and would I ever recommend divorce to a couple. I said that I never recommend divorce. That decision was the couple's alone. This answer did not please her. Her husband then remarked that he thought it was my duty as a Catholic to preserve their marriage, since divorce was not an option for them. I responded by saying that it was my responsibility to try to help them improve their relationship but not to keep their marriage together. These comments were followed by a brief silence. The couple then stood up. The wife called me a "heretic" and the couple left my office.

2. Kathy and Kevin were referred to me by their 9-year-old son's grade school teacher. Their son was chronically disruptive in class and difficult to manage at home. The boy's teacher said that she would be willing to work with me and his parents to help the child. Before seeing their son, I met Kathy and Kevin in order to gather information about his development and to take a history of the presenting problem. Kathy and Kevin wondered if their son might be suffering from attention deficit hyperactivity disorder (ADHD). I said that I could not make this determination without first evaluating him and having behavioral observations made in a number of key settings and environments. They added that even if their son were thought to have this condition, they were opposed to using psychotropic medication. I explained that my approach was to teach parents how to work as a team and to use a variety of child management techniques first. Then, if these proved unsuccessful, the parents might wish to consider other options. Kathy and Kevin were surprised to learn that they would be expected to become instrumentally involved in their son's assessment and treatment. Kevin then asked if the child management techniques I planned to teach them were "behavior modification." When I said that they were, Kathy said that she and Kevin were "humanists" and would never participate in what was considered to be the "dehumanizing practice of behavior modification." They thanked me for my time, said they would not feel comfortable using my approach, paid their bill, and left my office.

In the first example it is clear that the couple was threatened by the therapist, who would not take responsibility for ensuring that their marriage would not be dissolved. What these spouses wanted was for the therapist to give added strength and sanction to the barriers to divorce that made them feel safe and secure.

In the second example, Kathy and Kevin were frightened when it became clear that they would be required to work together and become significantly involved in their son's treatment. The triangulation and scapegoating of their son, which had served to stabilize their marriage, help them avoid open conflict, and regulate their interpersonal closeness was then turned against the therapist and used to terminate therapy.

Projection is central to scapegoating. The scapegoat becomes a repository for those aspects of both partners' selves that are unacceptable. When a child is the target, he or she often acts out for both parents. Therapists are usually surprised when they are scapegoated. They feel blindsided and wrongly accused. If the therapist becomes defensive or retaliates somehow, his or her response is seen as confirmation of the projected accusation. Stereotyping is another component of scapegoating. For Kathy and Kevin, anyone who used behavioral interventions was thought to adhere to a mechanistic philosophy of human development and behavior that was abhorrent to them. Even though this attribution was unfounded, it was all the couple needed to rationalize their decision to abort treatment. Sometimes there is some truth in the scapegoating accusations. Although it would be a far stretch to be considered a heretic, the couple in the first example did correctly intuit that I was not supportive of the Church's position concerning divorce.

Scapegoating and triangulation usually go hand in hand. In my work with families, I have found that these defensive dynamics are often transmitted intergenerationally. Couples who use them usually have experienced them at first hand in their families of origin. Genograms can be helpful in identifying these intergenerational patterns, thus alerting the therapist to their possible enactment if therapy becomes too threatening for the spouses.

STUDY QUESTIONS

1. In the case of Bill and Susan, the therapist directly addressed the couple's unverbalized and unacknowledged contractual rule for expressing negative feelings subtly through financial channels. The therapist made a clinical judgment that the couple would be receptive to such a direct interpretive approach. However if you, as this couple's therapist, judged that such a straightforward approach would be countertherapeutic, what are some other interventional strategies that could be used to address this collusive agreement?
2. In this chapter, two examples of client provocation were identified. One was negative and one positive in the form of flattery. Whereas a negative provocation may be fairly easy to identify, a positive provocation may be more difficult to recognize.

a. What other types of positive provocation have you encountered in your clinical work?
b. What countertransferential reactions were you able to recognize?
c. How long did it take you to realize that you might be responding countertransferentially?
d. What did you do once you understood what was happening?

Marital Structure, Interactive Dynamics, and the Self 2

As outlined in the introduction, an important function of marriage is reciprocal validation and protection of the partners' self-esteem. No matter how dysfunctional a marriage may appear to be from an outsider's perspective, it is assumed that reciprocal validation still exists to some degree, or else—unless it is perceived to be nonvoluntary by one or both spouses—the marriage would have been dissolved. When insurmountable barriers to divorce are perceived by dissatisfied spouses, a marriage is conceptualized as being nonvoluntary from a social exchange perspective (Levinger, 1976). Since no empirically developed instruments were available to assess barrier strength in marriages, my colleagues and I (Bagarozzi, 1983; Bagarozzi & Atilano, 1982; Bagarozzi & Pollane, 1983) developed a clinical instrument that therapists could use to identify spouses' perceptions of barriers to divorce and to assess the strength of these. The result was the Spousal Inventory of Desired Changes and Relationship Barriers (SIDCARB). SIDCARB comprises three empirically derived factor scales: Satisfaction with the Social Exchange Process in Ten Areas of Marital Exchange, Internal Psychological Barriers to Divorce, and External Circumstantial Barriers to Relationship Termination. A more thorough discussion of SIDCARB appears in Chapter 3. The importance of perceived barriers to divorce can explain why some severely distressed marriages endure in spite of the high degree of conflict, dissatisfaction, mutual punishment, and negative behavioral reciprocity, all of which would lead some clinical researchers to predict divorce (Gottman, 1994).

Barrier strength as measured by SIDCARB, however, does not explain why some spouses still remain in severely distressed and conflict-ridden marriages when neither spouse perceives the marriage to be nonvoluntary. One reason can be found in the implicit contracts that spouses may devise to validate their respective selves. The following example is illustrative.

Rodney was a tenured college professor who had a reputation for speaking his mind and making embarrassing and inappropriate comments at faculty meetings and social gatherings. His wife, Claire, routinely admonished him for his offensive comments, which were a constant source of friction between them. These conflicts escalated to a point where the couple found it necessary to seek professional assistance. Rodney and Claire's SIDCARB profile showed that neither spouse perceived their marriage to be nonvoluntary, but both reported moderate levels of dissatisfaction.

A close examination of the couple's relationship dynamics revealed that Claire's self-esteem was highly dependent on Rodney's troublesome behavior. The more he behaved badly in public, the more competent Claire appeared to sympathetic friends, neighbors, colleagues, relatives, and others. Even though Claire's criticism and disapproval of Rodney's behavior often led to conflicts between them, Rodney perceived her admonitions as demonstrations of love, caring, and concern for him—that is, they validated his self-worth and his persona as an eccentric college professor. Rodney was very successful in his ability to project this impression, thus keeping most people at a distance and protecting himself from having to engage in intimate relationships, which were frightening to him. Helping Rodney and Claire to develop less-corrosive ways to validate each other's selves was the focus of treatment with this couple.

VALIDATION OF THE NEGATIVE SELF

Sometimes, highly conflicted couples stay together voluntarily because doing so validates the negative self of one or both spouses. Conscious or unconscious shame and guilt frequently play a significant role in such marriages. The negative self may have its roots in feelings of unworthiness, incompetence, or in the belief that one is truly bad and deserving of punishment. In such cases, spouses may be chosen specifically because they will fulfill the role of punisher. Reciprocal negative exchanges and escalating conflicts having no resolution often characterize such relationships. Here again, such couples may seek treatment only when punishment, humiliation, violence, and so on exceed their mutually agreed upon contractual limits, which maintain dyadic equilibrium.

An understanding of the salient themes that play significant roles in their lives can often explain why some spouses voluntarily stay in conflict-ridden and dissatisfying marriages. Life themes exist at various levels of awareness. The sum total of an individual's life themes has been referred to as one's personal mythology (Anderson & Bagarozzi, 1983, 1988; Bagarozzi & Anderson, 1982, 1988, 1989). Life themes have their genesis in the experiences one has in his or her family of origin. Each developmental stage poses a number of challenges that must be confronted and resolved. Family of origin dynamics can facilitate or interfere with the successful resolution of these hierarchically ordered and invariantly sequenced developmental challenges. Unresolved developmental challenges persist as themes that press for successful resolution throughout later life. It is not unusual for a person to select a spouse with life themes that he or she believes will make it possible to replay, rework, and resolve these earlier conflicts through transference, projective identification, collusive acting out, monitoring, and restraining. Life themes of punishment, expiation, and atonement are common among individuals who see themselves as unworthy, incompetent, or bad. An example of two women with very similar life themes is presented below:

> Sheila was born and raised in a large urban area. Her parents provided little supervision, bordering on neglect. Although intellectually gifted and a superior student in high school, she thought of herself as unworthy and unlovable. By the time she reached the age of 24, she had had two abortions. Shame and guilt became driving forces in her life. She married a self-righteous man who considered himself to be morally superior to her. He took every opportunity that presented itself to demean Sheila and verbally abused her for the sordid life she led before he had "saved" her. Sheila described her marriage as a "self-imposed penance."
>
> Layla, like Sheila, had led a sexually promiscuous life before she married Paul, a successful businessman 8 years her senior. Paul was a kind, understanding fatherly figure. Unfortunately, Paul's unconditional acceptance and sympathetic understanding of Layla's past behavior was not what she desired, since it did not afford her the punishment she believed she deserved. In order to provoke Paul, Layla became involved in a fairly public extramarital affair, but this still did not produce the negative outcome she had hoped for. Paul's response to this affair was to suggest marital counseling.

Both Sheila and Layla were involved in voluntary marriages. The major difference, however, was that Sheila had married a man whose own life themes of righteous judge and jury were complementary to Sheila's need for punishment. It is instructive to note that Layla and Paul sought treatment for themselves. Sheila and her husband, on the other hand, sought treatment for their 13-year-old daughter, who, not surprisingly, had begun to act out sexually.

One's self-concept and one's perception of one's spouse will affect, to a large degree, how one treats his or her partner and how he or she expects to be treated in return. Table 2.1 presents 16 possible combinations of self/spouse perceptions

Table 2.1
Matrix of Self/Spouse Perceptions for Goodness and Badness

	Husband's perceptions of self/wife			
	1 G/G G/G	2 G/B G/G	3 B/G G/G	4 B/B G/G
Wife's perceptions of self/husband	5 G/G G/B	6 G/B G/B	7 B/G G/B	8 B/B G/B
	9 G/G B/G	10 G/B B/G	11 B/G B/G	12 B/B B/G
	13 G/G B/B	14 G/B B/B	15 B/G B/B	16 B/B B/B

G = Good
B = Bad

of goodness (Worthiness, Competence, Deserving Respect) and badness (Unworthiness, Incompetence, Undeserving of Respect) presented as ideal types. In section 1, for example, the top line shows the way the husband perceives himself and his wife; the line underneath shows the wife's perceptions of herself and her husband. When each spouse's perception of the voluntary/nonvoluntary nature of the marriage is also taken into consideration, insight into the couples' interactions and dynamics that goes beyond behavioral exchanges and negative reciprocity becomes possible. An assessment of a spouse's perceptions of his or her own worthiness and competence can be measured by using the Multidimensional Self-Esteem Inventory (O'Brien & Epstein, 1988). This measure is discussed in detail in Chapter 8. Estimations about spouses' evaluations of their partners' goodness or badness can be inferred from how the spouses treat one another. Self/spouse perceptions of Sheila's marriage are shown in Table 2.1, section 10. Those of Layla and Paul are represented in Table 2.1, section 9.

CONCEPTUALIZING THE SELF

The self is conceptualized as a superordinate structural system having cognitive and affective components that influence behavior at both the conscious and unconscious levels of awareness. The self's primary function is to organize one's experiences, both internal and external, into some coherent, meaningful whole. The self attempts to bring order into the individual's life. Although the self strives for wholeness and completeness, anxiety-producing experiences during critical periods of development, especially during the first few years of life, can seriously weaken, retard, or distort the self's progression toward cohesive integrity and stability. Trauma, empathic failure, and the absence of tenderness on the part of one's caretakers may so weaken the self's ability to master anxiety that cohesion suffers and the self becomes divided or fragmented.

The self as a discrete entity begins to emerge at the end of what Mahler (1968) refers to as the symbiotic stage of development. It is at this time that the infantile ego begins to develop in response to demands made by the external world. The infantile ego has two major developmental tasks to accomplish during this critical period: to help the child satisfy its basic physiological needs and to protect the fragile self from experiencing overwhelming anxiety. The first of these tasks is referred to as reality testing. Through this process the child begins to acquire rudimentary knowledge about the external world so that he or she can gradually develop the skills necessary to gain some degree of mastery and competence.

The second task entails the development and deployment of self-protective primitive defense mechanisms, such as hallucinatory wish fulfillment, magical thinking, denial, introjections, projection, primary identification, selective inattention, dissociation, apathy, and splitting. As the child develops, these primitive defenses will be replaced by higher-order defensive operations, unless constitutional factors or psychic trauma inhibits their acquisition or compromises their use later in life.

By the end of the first year of life, two additional developmental milestones should have been achieved—that is, the solidification of a cohesive and integrated self and the establishment of an enduring sense of trust, security, and safety with one's primary attachment figure. During the second year of life, separation-individuation is the critical task to be mastered. Discouragement of this budding autonomy by the withdrawal of love, tenderness, praise, and so on, or by direct punishment of the child's efforts to become more independent, can create severe anxiety, stress, fear, shame, and guilt, which can impede the child's progression toward separation-individuation as well as the development of self-esteem and a positive self-concept.

Early childhood ushers in what Sullivan (1953) calls the personified self. A central component of the personified self is the recognition and identification of one's gender as an integral part of the self. The solidification of one's gender identity during middle childhood is facilitated by interaction and association with same-sex peers. Within the context of the same-sex peer group, sex role behaviors, attitudes, beliefs, and gender-specific themes and scripts are reciprocally shaped and reinforced through interactive play. Sullivan (1953) postulates that these peer group experiences are critical to the establishment, stability, and continuity of a cohesive self. They also provide a very valuable extrafamilial source of self-esteem, identification, and the building of a more complex, multifaceted self.

The experience of being ostracized by one's peers during later childhood can have a devastating effect upon the developing self. Being shunned by one's peers can contribute significantly to one's feelings of alienation and difference. Being rejected by his or her peers may make it very difficult for the developing child to have the interpersonal experiences that are necessary to forming and maintaining close, intimate relationships later in life. For example, through competitive play with one's peers, feelings of adequacy and competence are enhanced. Being a member of a cohesive peer group also affords the child numerous opportunities to learn how to compromise, cooperate, and collaborate with others. The ability to compromise, cooperate, and collaborate is essential for the development of true intimacy. Being cut off from one's peers, therefore, can have serious implications for learning how to get along with one's spouse or partner, especially if such isolation continues throughout adolescence.

Being a member of a cohesive peer group during childhood does not ensure that one will be able to develop close and intimate relationships as an adult. The danger that threatens during this developmental stage is for competition to become the principal mode of relating to others and for competition to be used as a major defensive operation for protecting the self and gaining self-esteem. When being competitive becomes a person's predominant way of protecting the self and bolstering self-esteem, learning to compromise, cooperate, and collaborate may suffer considerably. If a competitive personality style becomes crystallized during adolescence, the capacity for intimacy with members of either sex will suffer.

According to Sullivan (1953), the need for intimacy, especially sexual intimacy, with members of the opposite sex distinguishes adolescence from all previous developmental stages. Integrating the various components of one's sexuality (affective, behavioral, cognitive, attitudinal, etc.) into a cohesive whole is a critical aspect of adolescent identity formation (Erikson, 1968, 1982). The danger that threatens during this developmental epoch is that desire for sexual gratification may dominate or supplant all other components of this basic need for interpersonal closeness and intimacy (Bagarozzi, 2001).

The achievement of a solid, enduring, and integrated identity makes it possible to develop mature and intimate adult relationships based upon mutual respect and trust. In such relationships, the true self is revealed.

THE IDEAL SELF

The development of one's self-concept depends, to a great degree, upon the interpersonal experiences one has had over a protracted period of time with primary attachment figures, caretakers, peers, and other individuals who are a central part of one's life. Through gradual identification with significant others, the developing child begins to see himself or herself through their eyes. This is when the child begins to develop a concept of what he or she should be or what he or she would like to become. This vision of one's possible self has both conscious and unconscious dimensions and has been referred to as one's ideal self. Given the person's innate abilities, talents, skills, physical characteristics, and so on, the ideal self can be realistic and attainable or unrealistic and unattainable. Self-esteem is dependent, to a large degree, upon one's ability to live up to this ideal. As was discussed in the introduction, self-esteem is made up of two interrelated components: worthiness and competence. Standards for judging one's worthiness and competence are represented in the ideal self. The more a person approximates these ideal standards, the greater will be his or her self-esteem. The more one fails to live up to these ideal standards, the more likely one will be to have low self-esteem and to suffer from depression.

Self-worth is communicated to the child verbally, nonverbally, consciously, and unconsciously by the way the child is treated, labeled, disciplined, and scripted by significant others. Under optimal conditions, the self is judged to be worthy, competent, and good; thus the ideal self is realistic and attainable. Under less-favorable circumstances, the self may be judged as conditionally worthy and competent, sometimes good and sometimes bad, and the ideal self may sometimes be attainable or sometimes out of reach, vague, or ambivalently conceptualized. Under the least desirable conditions, the self is judged to be unworthy and incompetent; thus, the ideal self is seen as representing a perfection that can never be attained. In a minority of cases, the person may strive to achieve an ideal self that is negative, bad, or evil. Frequently, this is the ideal self that one finds in many individuals who are diagnosed as having an antisocial personality disorder.

Once established, a person's self-concept is difficult to change, since the self strives for consistency and continuity. Therefore, the individual will tend to behave in ways that are congruent and consistent with his or her self-concept, especially when that self-concept and his or her ideal self are closely matched. Similarly, congruence, consistency, and continuity are also maintained by the person as he or she seeks self-confirmatory experiences, environments, and relationships—including marriage—that tend to reinforce, validate, affirm, and protect this self's definition, as in the cases of Sheila and Layla.

To obtain a more in-depth picture of a spouse's ideal self-concept, the following questions can be asked in the course of the history-taking process:

1. How do you think your mother felt when she learned that she was pregnant with you?
2. How do you think your father felt when he learned that your mother was pregnant with you?
3. How do you think your mother felt about your gender?
4. How do you think your father felt about your gender?

Probably one of the most significant self-evaluations after these judgments about one's goodness or badness is one's feelings about worthiness and competence as related to one's gender. The devaluing of one's gender by parents can have a devastating effect upon one's self-esteem. Such devaluation can be subtle or overt, as when children are dressed in the clothes of the opposite sex or given opposite-sex names.

5. What did you have to do in order to be loved by your mother?
6. What did you have to do in order to be loved by your father?

Questions 5 and 6 address the issues of conditional love and the sense of worthiness and competence in relation to the person's family of origin. The role that one is expected to play in one's family is frequently related to worthiness and competence. The more successful one is in fulfilling that role, the more competent and loved he or she will feel. Question 7 deals with this dynamic.

7. What was your role in your family and how successful were you in performing this role?

To answer this question, the respondent must be able to step back and consider his or her contribution to the overall family dynamic. This requires a certain degree of objectivity. Two additional issues must also be taken into account: how the person feels about the role he or she was expected to play and to what extent this role has become incorporated into the self, defining it.

8. Who was your mother's favorite family member, and what was it about this person that you believe made him or her your mother's favorite?
9. Who was your father's favorite family member, and what was it about this person that you believe made him or her your father's favorite?

The favorite family member may not be a sibling. Nevertheless, the person who is favored often becomes a significant component of one's ideal self—a model to be emulated and a standard for comparison. The closer one comes to achieving this ideal, the higher one's self-esteem will be. Failure to reach this ideal often leads to decreased self-esteem, sadness, and depression. I find it helpful to think about the two components of self-esteem (worthiness and competence) as having both trait and state dimensions—the former being fairly stable, the latter fluctuating within a given range for a particular person. To further profile a person's ideal self, the following questions can be used:

10. What personality traits were most valued by your mother?
11. What personality traits were most valued by your father?

Disciplinary practices target the self. How a child is disciplined communicates the disciplinarian's valuing of that child as predominantly good or bad, worthy or unworthy, competent or incompetent. It sets the stage for what the adult will accept as permissible treatment from others. Spouses' responses to questions 12, 13, and 14 can offer valuable insights into why some people stay in abusive relationships voluntarily.

12. What types of discipline did your mother use to correct your behavior?
13. What types of discipline did your father use to correct your behavior?
14. How did this discipline affect the way you felt about yourself and your parents?

The type of discipline used, its harshness and frequency, and the consistency with which it was applied all must be viewed within the context of the relationship that existed between the disciplinarian and the child during the critical years of self-formation. For example, discipline perceived as justified, fair, and appropriate—as applied by a parent whom the child views as loving and caring—will have a very different effect upon the developing self than will discipline that is seen as harsh, unfair, unjustified, and administered by a cold, distant, uncaring parent. Another important component of discipline that must be taken into account is the extent to which shaming and guilt-inducing disciplinary techniques were used. This distinction is an important one, since shaming targets the self, whereas guilt targets the child's behavior.

The final two questions deal with issues of validation and protection of the self:

15. What do you like most about yourself?
16. What do you like least about yourself?

In harmonious, satisfying, and successful marriages, spouses will validate, praise, and cherish the positive qualities and traits of their partners. In such relationships, as mentioned in the introduction, spouses will avoid doing or saying anything that would damage the defensive systems that their partners have erected—systems designed to protect those aspects of the self that are particularly vulnerable. In conflict-ridden marriages where punishment is deemed to be deserved, however, a spouse's positive qualities are often demeaned, derided, and mocked, negative qualities and traits are validated, and vulnerabilities are deliberately attacked.

The tactics used to punish one's spouse are frequently the same tactics the punishing spouse experienced himself or herself as a child. Projective identification is usually operating in such cases.

STUDY QUESTION

1. This chapter included a number of questions that therapists can use to gain some understanding of each spouse's self-concept. This list of questions is by no means exhaustive. Are there any additional questions that you believe would be important to include in order to get a more complete picture of a spouse's self-concept? List these additional questions below and explain why you believe each one to be relevant.

Assessment: Theoretical and Practical Considerations 3

The premise upon which the clinical approach outlined in this text rests is that the practice of marital therapy should be guided by a coherent theory of marital behavior and relationship development. This theory should explain how destructive interaction patterns and faulty relationship structures come into being and how they are maintained over time. Intervention strategies designed to correct these dysfunctional patterns and faulty structures should follow logically from the basic tenets and formulations of the theory concerning how change takes place and how change can be effected through planned therapeutic action. Instruments, measures, tests, and procedures chosen for diagnostic assessment and post-treatment evaluation should be theory-derived and problem-focused whenever feasible.

THEORETICAL FORMULATIONS

The approach to the short-term problem-focused treatments described in this volume is best described as integrative. Three theoretical perspectives are woven together in order to provide a multifaceted view of dyadic interaction. These three are social exchange theory, psychodynamic/object relations theory, and marital/family systems theory.

Social Exchange Formulations Concerning Marriage and Other Intimate Dyadic Relationships

Sociologists and social psychologists were among the first to explain the dynamics of dyadic interaction in terms of social exchange behaviors and expectations between participants in intimate relationships. Thibaut and Kelley (1959), Adams (1963, 1965), and Homans (1974) postulated that people will voluntarily remain in intimate relationships only as long as the exchanges between the partners are perceived to be fair, equitable, and more rewarding than costly and that there are no better alternatives promising greater rewards and satisfactions.

Family theorists have also proposed theories of marriages based upon the idea of social exchanges between spouses (Blood & Wolfe, 1960; Edwards, 1969; Waller & Hill, 1951). The perception of inequities in the exchange process between spouses is considered by these theorists to be a major cause of marital dissatisfaction and distress. The perception of continued inequitable exchanges between spouses disrupts the couple's equilibrium. Overt conflicts develop when spouses use punishment and other coercive means in their attempts to reestablish the previously existing balance of exchanges. Although one might expect marriages to be dissolved when exchange inequities persist, this is often not the case. Levinger (1976) outlined several factors that might prevent the termination of dissatisfying marriages characterized by gross inequities in the marital exchange process. These include the presence of children; commitment to marriage vows; religious beliefs; affiliation with primary groups such as parents, in-laws, friends, and neighbors; and, finally, legal, economic, and financial considerations. Such marriages have been termed nonvoluntary (Bagarozzi & Wodarski, 1977). In some cases, these marriages may evidence all the ingredients of a double-bind relationship (Bateson, Jackson, Haley, & Weakland, 1956).

Psychodynamic and Object Relations Conceptualizations Regarding Marital Contracts and Exchanges Between Spouses

Some exchange expectations in marriage are not often verbalized by spouses or articulated clearly when they are violated. Usually, they take the form of Sager's (1976) level II quid pro quo contractual expectations—that is, those that are consciously or preconsciously recognized but not openly discussed and negotiated. Sager's (1976) level III contract expectations are those that are beyond awareness and are unconsciously negotiated, very much like Dicks's (1967) formulations. Dicks (1967), however, focuses on the psychological mechanisms and defensive operations used to stabilize these unconscious contractual agreements. These approaches have much in common and are considered to be complementary.

The Systems Perspective

As with social exchange and psychodynamic/object relations conceptualizations of marriage and intimate partnerships, systems theorists also focus on contractual exchanges and agreements between spouses. Haley (1963) states that the working out of a marital relationship can best be described as a process of negotiating contractual rules for living together as a couple. This process also determines which spouse will make the rules governing the couple's exchanges and, in a larger sense, the couple's relationship in general. The former set of rules has to do with justice, equity, fairness, and reciprocity; the latter set has to do with power, dominance, and control in the relationship. For Haley (1963), the more easily resolved contractual disagreements have to do with the rules of exchange. More serious difficulties that manifest themselves in the form of emotional fights between partners have to do with who will make the rules for living together as a couple. Struggles over who will make the rules are so intense because they deal with dominance, power, and control; therefore, they pose a serious threat to autonomy and the integrity of the self.

Theoretical Integration

What ties all three theoretical perspectives together in a meaningful way and makes coherent integration possible is the shared theoretical premise that marriages and all intimate relationships are contractually negotiated rule-governed systems. Therefore, an important assessment task for the therapist is to determine what contractual rules have been violated or no longer serve their original purpose. Next, the therapist must try to determine how the breakdown in the couple's rule system manifests itself in the form of the presenting problem, since helping the couple to develop a more satisfying and functional set of rules is the focal point of treatment. The determination process begins in the first session, when the couple is asked to respond to and discuss a number of questions related to the presenting problem. The answers to these questions and how the couple interacts while discussing them offer the therapist an excellent opportunity to observe how the couple deals with exchange conflicts and power sharing in their relationship. The first six questions are addressed to the couple as a unit and not to a particular spouse:

1. It will be helpful if you tell me what problem or problems in your relationship have caused you to seek my professional help?
2. How long has this problem or conflict existed between the two of you?

3. What have you done in the past to solve the problem or resolve the conflict?
4. What procedures have been helpful?
5. What procedures have not been very helpful?
6. Why have you decided to seek professional help at this time in your relationship?

The next two questions are addressed to each spouse/partner in turn:

7. What have you done personally to solve your problem or to correct the situation?
8. Do you think your efforts to deal with this problem have been successful, or have they made the problem worse?

Finally, the couple are asked to agree upon specific treatment goals and outcomes. The following questions are posed:

9. What do you hope to accomplish in therapy? Be as behaviorally specific as you can.
10. If therapy were to be successful, what would your marriage/relationship look like at the end of treatment?
11. Is there anything else about your problem that you think would be important for me to know that we have not discussed so far? If yes, let's talk about it.
12. Is there anything else about your relationship that you think would be important for me to know in order to help you? If yes, explain.

At the close of the first session, two separate individual interviews are scheduled for each partner/spouse. Although some therapists may not wish to conduct individual assessment and diagnostic interviews, I have found that the material gathered in such interviews often reveals important information that may be crucial to treatment success but may never come to light in the context of short-term problem-focused therapy. For example, a couple came to see me for help with "communication problems" in their marriage. The goal was improved communication. During her individual session, the wife casually mentioned that she would sometimes have a "little bed-wetting accident." This did not seem to bother her very much, and she said that her husband was sympathetic and understanding. When I questioned her more closely about her bed-wetting, it became clear that her "accidents" sometimes occurred after a disagreement had taken place between the spouses. The retaliatory aspect of her bed-wetting and the controlling nature of this symptom were obvious, but the husband's nonchalant acceptance of it was curious. During one of his individual sessions, the husband brought up his wife's bed-wetting and his response to it as an example of how accepting and supportive he was as a husband. As we talked, it became clear that this supportive and "parental" role was a major source of the husband's self-esteem. Had individual interviews not been conducted, this symptom might have remained hidden and the role it played in the couple's relationship would have gone unnoticed. Unwittingly, the couple had called attention to their mutually protective collusive contractual agreement, which allowed them to prevent serious marital conflicts over the control of their relationship.

Individual interviews are also used to arrive at diagnoses. Here again, identification of a psychiatric symptom or a personality disorder that otherwise might have gone unnoticed is made easier in a one-on-one setting, as is the identification of individual defense mechanisms. Personal and family of origin histories are also gathered during these individual sessions. Such interviews provide valuable insights into significant roles, scripts, conflicts, life themes, and so on that have played a part in shaping each spouse's/partner's self-definition, ideal self, and level of self-esteem.

SELECTION OF ASSESSMENT INSTRUMENTS

At the beginning of this chapter, the importance of theoretically grounded, empirically based instruments for the purpose of pretreatment assessment and post-treatment evaluation was stressed. Routinely, a battery of such tests and instruments is used to help the couple and the therapist identify salient treatment issues and to formulate agreed-upon treatment goals. Three categories of instruments are included in this battery. The first category is best characterized as being generic, in that the measures employed are not theory-specific but can be used to assess universal aspects of marital relationships, such as adjustment and satisfaction. Such measures can often be used as global assessments of treatment outcomes and effectiveness. The second category consists of theory-derived instruments that have been developed to assess specific theoretical constructs believed to be central to successful marital functioning and relationship satisfaction. The final category is made up of empirically developed instruments and tests that target a specific relationship problem. These instruments and tests may or may not have a theoretical underpinning derived from a particular school of marital/family process and/or therapy. Nevertheless, they can provide the therapist with valuable information and can often be used as measures of therapeutic gain and success.

Category I: Generic Measures of Adjustment and Satisfaction

There literally are scores of reliable and valid measures of marital satisfaction and adjustment. For a review and catalogue of the numerous instruments, tests, procedures, and so forth that are available to assess marital adjustment and satisfaction, the interested reader should consult Touliatos, Perlmutter, and Holden (2001), and Touliatos, Perlmutter, and Straus (2001).

The most widely used but by no means most recently developed measure of marital adjustment is the Dyadic Adjustment Scale, or DAS (Spanier, 1976; Spanier & Thompson, 1982). The DAS has been employed in more than a thousand studies and is considered to be the criterion measure in the field of family studies; it is often used as a pretreatment/post-treatment measure of therapeutic effectiveness. The DAS, a 32-item questionnaire that utilizes a Likert-type format, was designed to assess relational quality as perceived by spouses. It can be employed as a general measure of marital adjustment by using total scores, or its four subscales can be used to assess couple cohesion, consensus, satisfaction, and expression of affection. Reliabilities for these subscales range from 0.73 to 0.90. This self-report instrument can be completed in 5 to 10 minutes and hand-scored within approximately the same amount of time. A shorter 14-item version, the Adapted Dyadic Adjustment Scale (Busby, Christiansen, Crane, & Larson, 1995; Crane, Middleton, & Bean, 2000), has been developed specifically for clinical use.

The Lock-Wallace Marital Adjustment Test, or LWMAT (Locke & Wallace, 1959), was developed to provide a valid, reliable measure of marital adjustment; it has set the standard for the measurement of this construct. These researchers defined marital adjustment as the "accommodation of a husband and wife to each other at a given time" in the couple's relationship. What many people do not know about the LWMAT is that 11 of the items that Spanier (1976) used in constructing the DAS were reproduced verbatim from the former instrument. The inclusion of these 11 items most likely accounts for the high correlations between these two instruments (e.g., 0.86-0.93) reported in various studies. The LWMAT was also used as the source of concurrent validity for the DAS.

In my clinical work, I often use both measures, because the LWMAT contains some unique items not included in the DAS and also addresses some important issues that the DAS and other similar instruments do not. If brevity is required, however, therapists might consider using the three-item Kansas Marital Satisfaction Scale (Schumm, Jurich, & Bollman, 1981).

Category II: Theoretically Derived Instruments

Spousal Inventory of Desired Changes and Relationship Barriers (SIDCARB)

The Spousal Inventory of Desired Changes and Relationship Barriers, or SIDCARB (Bagarozzi, 1983; Bagarozzi & Atilano, 1982; Bagarozzi & Pollane, 1983), was developed to assess spouses' perceptions of their marriage from a social exchange theoretical perspective. SIDCARB was discussed briefly in the previous chapter, but a more detailed discussion of this measure and how it is used in treatment is warranted. Essentially, SIDCARB was designed to assess the three major components of the conjugal exchange process, as put forth by exchange theorists. These are (a) satisfaction with the current exchange arrangements in the marriage, (b) commitment to the marriage, and (c) barriers to relationship termination. The degree to which perceived alternative sources of satisfaction affect commitment to the relationship is inferred from the strength of perceived barriers to divorce. Three subscales derived from factor analysis were produced:

1. Dissatisfaction with the current exchange arrangement in the marriage, the strength of commitment to one's spouse, and the extent to which changes in a spouse's behavior is desired in ten areas of conjugal exchange (household chores, finances, communication, in-laws, religion, recreation, sexual relations, love and affection, friendships, and children).
2. How commitment to the marriage is affected by the spouse's perception of internal psychological barriers to divorce (obligations to children, commitment to marriage vows, religious beliefs, and sanctions from family).
3. How commitment to the marriage is affected by the spouse's perception of external circumstantial barriers to divorce (financial considerations, legal costs, job-related factors, and sanctions from friends and neighbors).

When spouses' scores for each of these three factors are compared and juxtaposed, the degree to which each spouse perceives the marriage to be voluntary/nonvoluntary can be determined. Seven different perceptions of marriage are possible. These are presented as ideal types:

1. Satisfying, voluntary, few or low barriers to divorce and committed to the marriage
2. Unsatisfying, voluntary, few or low barriers to divorce and committed to improving the marriage

3. Unsatisfying, voluntary, few or low barriers to divorce, not committed to improving the marriage, but no better alternatives are perceived to be available
4. Unsatisfying, voluntary, few or low barriers to divorce, not committed to improving the marriage, and better alternatives are perceived to be available
5. Satisfying, nonvoluntary, medium to high barriers to divorce, but committed to the marriage
6. Unsatisfying, nonvoluntary, medium to high barriers to divorce, but not committed to improving the marriage
7. Unsatisfying, nonvoluntary, medium to high barriers to divorce but committed to improving the marriage

Reliabilities for each of the empirically derived factor subscales are 0.86, 0.74, and 0.80 for factors I, II, and III, respectively. Standard scores were devised for each subscale. Each subscale has a mean of 50 and a standard deviation of 10.

Some examples of possible SIDCARB profiles are presented below for illustrative purposes.

Example I

Factor	H	W
I	56	55
II	48	51
III	52	53

This is a profile rarely seen in the therapist's office. It depicts a marriage where both spouses perceive their relationship to be satisfying and voluntary, with virtually no barriers to divorce.

Example II

Factor	H	W
I	60	66
II	52	56
III	62	63

This SIDCARB profile shows a marriage in which both spouses are experiencing some degree of dissatisfaction, with medium-strength external circumstantial barriers.

Example III

Factor	H	W
I	60	75
II	53	65
III	55	70

In this example, the wife is clearly distressed and perceives herself to be in a nonvoluntary marriage. Her husband, on the other hand, is not distressed and sees himself to be in a voluntary relationship. Because of his ability to leave the marriage, he has much more power than his wife. Research findings (Bagarozzi, 1990) have given support to strategic therapists' contention (Haley, 1963) that spouses who perceive themselves to have little or no power in a relationship from which there is no escape will be more likely to develop a psychiatric symptom as a countercontrol measure. Example III above depicts such a relationship.

Example IV

Factor	H	W
I	65	72
II	67	65
III	70	69

In this final example, we have a couple where both spouses are highly distressed and dissatisfied and both perceive their marriage to be nonvoluntary. In some marriages, such an arrangement may play out as a standoff between spouses, with neither giving in, especially if each partner knows how the other perceives the relationship. For some couples, however, knowing that there is no way out may serve as impetus to improving their relationship.

One of the drawbacks of SIDCARB is that it was developed to assess traditional heterosexual marriages and, therefore, was not suitable for homosexual relationships. With the advent of homosexual marriages and adoptions, however, it would not be surprising to find that barriers to relationship terminations that were thought to apply only to traditional heterosexual marriages were also relevant to homosexual unions.

Intimacy Needs Questionnaire

Satisfaction with intimate exchanges between spouses and partners also formed the basis for the development of the Intimacy Needs Questionnaire (Bagarozzi,

1990, 2001). This instrument can be used to assess the complex dynamics of intimacy in all types of relationships and is not limited to traditional marriages or heterosexual unions.

Intimacy is conceptualized as a basic human need. It is not merely something that one "wants" or "desires." It is a true human need that has its roots in and grows out of a more fundamental survival need for attachment. This biologically based need differs in strength from individual to individual and is thought to remain fairly stable throughout the course of a person's life.

The Intimacy Needs Questionnaire was designed to capture the reciprocal and interactive nature of the construct, which is conceptualized as having eight components: emotional, psychological, intellectual, sexual, physical (nonsexual), spiritual, esthetic, and social/recreational. The amount of time, on a daily basis, that one needs to feel intimately connected with a partner is considered separately. Each component of intimacy is assessed from two vantage points: receptivity and reciprocity.

Intimacy is based upon mutual trust, acceptance, and respect. Each partner must feel fully secure in sharing his or her deepest thoughts, feelings, desires, and so forth with his or her significant other without fear of being judged, ridiculed, or punished. In addition to knowing that one's partner knows, understands, accepts, and is receptive to whatever is shared and disclosed, each partner must feel and perceive that his or her mate is reciprocating (giving back in return) similar levels of self-disclosure and self-revelation, since reciprocity is at the heart of the exchange process.

Respondents are asked to evaluate the strength of their own needs, the partner's ability to meet and satisfy each need, and the partner's ability to be reciprocally responsive and intimate in each of the eight areas. Total needs strength scores for individuals range from 8 to 800. Average scores for individuals seen in therapy range from 450 to 650. The Intimacy Needs Questionnaire is still in its development stage, so no data for reliability or validity are available. Data collection is in progress but has not yet been completed. At present, the Intimacy Needs Questionnaire should be considered a clinical aid, the empirical status of which has yet to be determined.

Images

Images (Anderson, Bagarozzi, & Giddings, 1986) is a 35-item empirically derived instrument comprising seven factor analytically produced subscales that can be used in a variety of ways, depending upon the therapist's need and clinical orientation. These subscales are emotional gratification and support; sex-role orientation and physical attraction; sexual, emotional, and psychological gratification; parent and sibling identification; emotional maturity; intelligence; and homogamy.

Perceived Spouse/Ideal Spouse Discrepancies

Just as one's self-esteem is influenced to some degree by how the perceived self compares with the ideal self, satisfaction with one's spouse also depends to a large extent upon how closely one's partner is thought to approximate one's ideal mate. The Images instrument asks spouses to make perceived/ideal comparisons of their mates in terms of the 35 exchange items included in this measure. The greater the discrepancy between perceived/ideal ratings, the less satisfied an individual will tend to be with his or her spouse. Perceived spouse/ideal spouse item discrepancies are then targeted for discussion. It is not necessary to interpret the factor structure to couple.

Images and Validation of the Self

Several items included in this scale also can be used to assess the extent to which the respondent feels validated by his or her spouse. Some of these items are listed below.

> Item 1: "My spouse encourages me to grow and to be myself."
> Item 8: "My spouse is empathic and knows how I feel."
> Item 9: "My spouse treats me as a husband/wife should be treated."

Item 9 is purposefully vague in its wording in order to determine whether a spouse's treatment of the respondent is considered to be deserved and appropriate or undeserved and inappropriate. It will be recalled from Chapter 2 that Sheila and Layla expected to be treated poorly by their husbands. Such treatment would validate a negative or bad self-concept and would be considered deserved and appropriate by both women.

Psychodynamic Object Relations and Transferential Considerations

IMAGES

The Images instrument was not designed to assess unconscious processes per se, but spouses' responses to four questions can provide the therapist with some insight into the possible transferential dynamics that might be part of a couple's collusive contractual agreements (Dicks, 1967; Sager, 1976):

> Item 18: "My spouse is very much like my mother."
> Item 19: "My spouse is very much like my father."

Item 20: "My spouse is very much like my sister."

Item 21: "My spouse is very much like my brother."

The 35 items that make up the Images scale were reduced through factor analysis from 47 behaviorally worded statements derived from an extensive review of published and unpublished research studies related to mate selection, marital satisfaction, marital quality, and marital adjustment (Lewis & Spanier, 1979). These items covered a wide variety of content domains having to do with socioeconomic variables, factors related to interpersonal attraction, personality traits, attitudes concerning personal values, expectations of one's spouse, maturity, and interpersonal behavioral and conjugal interaction. In my work with Images, as mentioned earlier, it seemed less confusing for couples to discuss discrepancies item by item rather than focusing on items as components of a particular factor.

Chronbach's reliabilities for the seven factors range from 0.70 to 0.87.

Category III: Problem-Focused Instruments

Marital Disaffection Scale

The Marital Disaffection Scale (Kayser, 1996) is a 21-item Likert-type questionnaire. Marital disaffection is defined as a gradual loss of emotional attachment, a decline in caring about one's partner, emotional estrangement, and a sense of apathy and indifference toward one's spouse. Scores range from 21 to 84; the higher the score, the higher the disaffection. In my clinical experience, I have found that high disaffection scores are typical for spouses who are not motivated to enter therapy and are characteristic of spouses who are more likely to discontinue treatment once it has gotten under way. Depression and hypoactive sexual desire are not uncommon for disaffected spouses, especially if they perceive their marriage to be nonvoluntary. Divorce may become a viable option for highly disaffected spouses who perceive few or low barriers to relationship termination.

In two separate studies alphas were 0.95 and 0.97. Concurrent validity with the Snyder and Regts (1982) Scale of Disaffection was 0.93.

Trust Scale

The Trust Scale (Rempel, Holmes, & Zanna, 1985) measures three factor analytically derived components of this construct: predictability, dependability, and faith in one's partner. There are 17 items. Five items assess predictability, five items measure dependability, and the final seven items are devoted to faith. Item-total correlations within each subscale range from 0.33 to 0.58 for predictability, 0.35 to 0.59 for dependability, and 0.43 to 0.60 for faith. Factor loadings range from 0.43 to 0.84.

Many couples find it helpful to think about trust as a multifaceted construct, each having specific behavioral components that can become the focus of treatment. Conceptualizing trust in this manner is very compatible with a social exchange contractual approach to therapy.

The rebuilding of trust between partners is crucial to the successful outcome of therapy. This is especially true when infidelity is the presenting problem (Bagarozzi, 2008).

The focus of this chapter has been to demonstrate how theory, assessment, and practice are tied together. The reader should not come away with the impression that the assessment procedures and instruments selected for inclusion are the only ones that are appropriate for use by all clinicians. They simply represent *this* author's theoretical approach to conducting short-term integrative treatment. It is assumed that therapists who subscribe to other schools of intervention will use assessment procedures, measures, tests, and so forth that are consistent with their particular theoretical/clinical orientations. Similarly, the strategies used to deal with the various types of collusion presented in this volume represent *this* author's personal style of doing short-term problem-focused integrative therapy. Some readers may find these strategies to be compatible with their own styles and others may not, but style is not the issue. What is important is the ability to identify couples' collusions in their various forms and guises and to understand the purposes they serve. How therapists deal with such defensive systems is truly the artistry of therapy, and this cannot be derived from a book.

STUDY QUESTIONS

1. What theoretical orientation best describes the way you conceptualize marital/dyadic relationship dynamics?
2. When you consider your theoretical orientation, can you identify any tests, measures, instruments, procedures, and so on that are compatible with this orientation and are practical for use in your clinical work? List them below.
3. How comfortable are you using tests and measures for pretreatment assessments and post-treatment evaluations? Explain the reasons for your decision.

Revisiting the Presenting Problem as a Collusive Defense: Treatment Guidelines and Case Studies

4

It would be erroneous to assume that all presenting problems for which couples enter treatment represent a collusive defense, but the therapist should consider that such might be the case for some. Pretreatment assessments, personal histories, and each spouse's version of the couple's relationship history can help the therapist make this determination in many cases. Sometimes the couple's core issues and conflicts (which the presenting problem is meant to conceal) may not become apparent until the couple has been in treatment for some time. Whenever it is determined that the presenting problem is indeed a collusive defense, the therapist must decide how to proceed. The following two case examples offer some suggestions for dealing with this very sensitive issue.

WADE AND LOUISE

This couple was referred by their neighbors, who had consulted me for marital therapy several years earlier. Wade called for help with his wife, Louise, who was "stressed out" about her relationship with her mother. Wade explained that Louise and her mother had always had a "complicated" relationship but that it had become increasingly stressful since the birth of their daughter, Kathy, and the death of Louise's father several months after Kathy was born. When asked if he could describe the nature of the relationship between mother and daughter, Wade said that Louise's mother had always been a dominant force in her life but that her influence had been tempered, to some degree, by Louise's father. After the father's death, the buffer between the two women was removed and Louise called upon her husband to fulfill her father's role. Wade was uncomfortable with this assignment. His refusal to take on this responsibility was a source of conflict between him and Louise. Dealing with Louise's mother was considered to be the main (presenting) problem for this couple.

Assessment Summary

Both Wade's score and Louise's score on the Marital Adjustment Test were in the adjusted range. The only area where both spouses identified conflict was in "ways of dealing with in-laws." SIDCARB profiles for Wade and Louise were similar. They perceived their marriage to be satisfying and voluntary. Here again, the only area where conflicts surfaced for the couple was in dealing with in-laws. Disaffection scores for Wade and Louise were low, signifying a strong affectional bond. Very few "ideal spouse-perceived spouse" discrepancies were recorded for both on the IMAGES measure. Those that were identified had to do with disagreements about the expectation that Louise had for Wade's role as a husband vis-à-vis her mother. Trust, for Wade, was not an issue. However, Louise did register some misgivings on the "faith and dependability" subscales of this measure. Her concerns had to do with what she perceived to be Wade's lack of support and understanding about her need for him to act as a buffer between herself and her mother.

Wade and Louise both scored within the average range of total intimacy needs strength scores, but Wade's 560 score was considerably lower than Louise's score of 640.

Differences in total intimacy needs strength scores between spouses on the Intimacy Needs Questionnaire are not uncommon and should not be considered a major concern (Bagarozzi, 2001). However, a difference of 150 points or more is usually problematic. Intimacy problems can still occur even when two spouses have very similar total intimacy needs strength scores since the strengths of their component needs may differ greatly. Finally, dissatisfaction can still arise even when both partners have very similar Component Needs Strengths scores if receptivity and/or reciprocity transactions are deemed to be inadequate. For Louise, Wade was experienced as not being able to meet her emotional and psychological needs for both types of transactions, that is, receptivity and reciprocity. This dissatisfaction was exacerbated by the fact that Louise's needs for emotional and psychological intimacy were considerably stronger than her husband's.

Owing to the nature of the presenting problem, the Personal Authority in the Family Systems Questionnaire (Bray, Williamson, & Malone, 1984) was also administered. Louise's scores were high for the following subscales: intergenerational fusion, intergenerational intimidation, and personal authority. Wade's scores for all eight subscales were within the average range.

Feedback Session: Interpretation of Assessment Findings and Formulation of Treatment Goals

Wade and Louise were told that according to the way they both responded to the assessment questionnaires, their marriage appeared to be "solid" and "satisfying for the most part," but that there were a few issues of concern. I said that these issues seemed to be related to the couple's presenting problem: Louise's difficult relationship with her mother. The couple agreed with the interpretation that Louise's problems with her mother were having a negative impact upon their marriage. I added, however, that the person primarily responsible for dealing with Louise's mother was Louise herself and not Wade. In response to these remarks, Wade seemed relieved. Louise, on the other hand, was visibly distressed. She said that she had struggled most of her life to free herself from her mother's domination and that she never would have been allowed to date and marry Wade if it had not been for her father's intervention (a fact revealed during her individual interviews). Wade agreed that Louise's father had made it possible for the couple to marry. I told Louise that I could understand how difficult and frightening my recommendations sounded. I then referred to items on the Personal Authority in the Family Systems Questionnaire having to do with intergenerational fusion, intergenerational intimidation, and personal authority. I explained that each of these problematic items could be dealt with separately and gradually over time and that I could help her to become more assertive and competent in her dealings with her mother. I ended by saying that Wade's role in this process would be a supportive one. He would become her coach and would always be there for her on the sidelines whenever she needed him.

Louise said she needed some time to think about my suggestions before making a decision. The following week she and Wade returned, having decided to go forward with my proposal. They had no difficulty learning the communication skills that are the basis of successful problem-solving and conflict negotiation. This having been done, Wade and Louise were ready to develop strategies for dealing with Louise's mother's intrusiveness. Therapy proceeded as outlined below.

With Wade's input and support, Louise reviewed all the items she had identified as problematic regarding "personal authority" in the Family Systems Questionnaire. She then was asked to rank these items in terms of how difficult and threatening she thought it would be to tackle each item. Once all items had been ranked from least difficult and threatening to most difficult and threatening, a homework assignment was given. The couple was asked to come back to their next session prepared to address those items that Louise believed she could handle with the least amount of stress.

At the beginning of the following session, assertive responding techniques specifically designed to address the items identified by the couple were taught and practiced. Next, role plays were developed where Wade played the part of Louise's mother and I modeled the role Wade was to play as Louise's supportive coach. Once Louise felt confident that she would be able to interact with her mother more competently around these issues, the couple implemented the techniques they had practiced in their next encounter with Louise's mother.

Therapy continued along these lines for several weeks and Louise's confidence began to grow, but Wade seemed to become less engaged in therapy. On two occasions he suggested that Louise might come to their session without him since some last-minute business had come up at work and it was too late to reschedule their appointments. Something had disturbed the couple's equilibrium, but I was not sure what it might be. This became evident a short time later when Wade jokingly mentioned that therapy was becoming very time-consuming. When I asked him what he meant by this remark, he said that it was not the therapy per se but the amount of time the couple was spending practicing their communication skills and devising strategies to deal with Louise's mother. Louise added that Wade had been working overtime more frequently than he had in the past. She said that Wade owned the business and there was no reason for him to put in extra time, since there were a number of employees who could have done the work just as competently. As the couple continued to discuss this issue, it became clear that Wade was progressively withdrawing from Louise.

The Underlying Conflict and Contractual Violation

As treatment progressed, Louise became more proficient in setting limits and managing her mother's intrusiveness, but she also began to rely more heavily upon Wade for emotional and psychological support. This made Wade uncomfortable, since his needs for intimacy in these two areas were considerably lower than Louise's. In the past, Louise's father had been her emotional and psychological support. Wade played only an ancillary role in this regard. Louise's relationship with her mother was not completely negative, and she did provide Louise with some measure of psychological and emotional intimacy. However, Louise soon realized that when she sought her mother's support, she was also opening the door for her mother's intrusions. She decided that she would no longer confide in her mother about issues of substance and turned to Wade.

Louise was unilaterally changing the couple's unacknowledged intimacy contract. Louise's father served as a buffer not only between Louise and her mother but also between Louise and Wade. Similarly, the more successful Louise was in managing her mother, the less she became the target of scapegoating and triangulation between the spouses. The couple was then faced with their underlying conflict over intimacy.

Wade's inability to fulfill Louise's needs for psychological and emotional intimacy caused him to feel inadequate and incompetent. He withdrew to an area where he felt safe, useful, competent, and in control—his business.

Revising the Treatment Contract to Deal With the Underlying Issues

During the session following the one in which Wade had remarked that therapy was becoming very time-consuming, I asked the couple to evaluate their progress and to assess how successful they had been in resolving their presenting problem. Both Wade and Louise said that they were pleased with the progress they had made as a team and in dealing with Louise's mother. Louise, however, said that she believed the problem was not completely solved and that more work needed to be done. She added that she was not ready to end therapy. Wade agreed but suggested that Louise continue therapy without him. He said he would still be able to act as Louise's coach but saw no need to attend the weekly sessions. I asked Louise what she thought and felt about Wade's proposal. She responded by saying that she wanted him to continue to come to sessions with her.

Wade's suggestion can be interpreted as his attempt to return to a time when the couple's equilibrium was maintained by Louise's father, acting as a buffer between Louise and her mother and Louise and Wade. I did not offer this interpretation to the couple; instead, I merely said that I considered Wade to be an essential part of the process and thought it would be beneficial for the couple, not just Louise, if he continued. Wade then agreed to continue.

At the beginning of the next session, I asked Louise to discuss, more precisely, what further work she thought needed to be done in therapy. She said that now that her mother had become less of a distraction, it would be nice if she and Wade could rejuvenate their relationship—she hoped that they could "reconnect." Wade was less than enthusiastic when I asked him how he felt about Louise's comments. He said that it sounded "good," but quickly added that it was a very busy time of year for his business and that he did not know how much time he could devote to "reconnecting" at the moment. I then asked Louise how she envisioned this reconnection. She said that it was not so much the amount of time the couple spent together but how they spent that time that was the issue. Wade was silent, but, when I asked him if he would like to "go down this path," said he would do the best he could.

The question to be answered was: Would the couple be able to develop a level of intimacy that would satisfy Louise's needs for emotional and psychological support and also enhance Wade's feelings of competence and adequacy as a husband?

I said that I thought it might be fruitful to begin this process of reconnecting by reviewing the Intimacy Needs Questionnaire, since this instrument could be considered a measure of connectedness. The couple agreed.

As mentioned earlier, differences in the strengths of the same component need are not in themselves problematic, since receptivity and reciprocity satisfaction are subjective. Spouses may have very different needs strengths but still experience their needs as being met satisfactorily by their partners. Receptivity and reciprocity scores that fall below a 70% satisfaction level are considered to be a matter of concern. Receptivity and reciprocity satisfaction scores for Louise on both subscale components (psychological intimacy and emotional intimacy) were in the 60% range. These scores are not extreme and could be improved with some work. This was the interpretation given to Wade and Louise when we reviewed the instrument. Wade found these remarks to be encouraging.

Receptivity satisfaction is usually easier to improve if spouses are able to learn the reflective listening skills taught at the outset of therapy. Reciprocity satisfaction is more difficult to achieve, since it requires intimate disclosures that leave the self vulnerable. Here again, however, the degree of self-disclosure deemed necessary for satisfaction is subjective. As we reviewed Louise's scores on the Intimacy Needs Questionnaire, she said that she felt that Wade had become more receptive to her, in general. His receptivity was no longer an issue for her. Reciprocity, in these two areas, was still perceived as falling short of the mark. Improving reciprocity satisfaction for Louise now became the focus of treatment.

INTERVENTION

Wade's uneasiness with self-disclosure was a major stumbling block to reciprocity satisfaction for Louise. In order to overcome this obstacle, Wade was taught to use a number of self-disclosure communication techniques that posed very little threat to the self. These are discussed below.

1. *Affirmative Expressive Concordance*—There are two components to this: agreement and reciprocal sharing of feelings. The respondent is taught to express his or her agreement with the sentiments and feelings expressed by the speaker when agreement is genuine. He or she then expresses the same or very similar feelings concerning the issue being discussed.
2. *Neutral or Nondefensive Acknowledgment*—This technique is used to respond to statements or assertions made by the speaker when agreement would be inappropriate, not genuine, or insincere. The respondent simply acknowledges the speaker's perception, feelings, viewpoints, and so on and expresses his or her understanding of (but not agreement with) the speaker's position. If the respondent strongly disagrees with the viewpoints or opinions put forth by the speaker, he or she may decide to offer an opposing or different view in a noncombative, nonconfrontational manner.
3. *Sympathetic Sharing*—The expression of genuine feelings of caring and affiliation is at the heart of sympathetic sharing. In response to the speaker, the respondent may express his or her feelings of sadness, sorrow, concern, joy, happiness, excitement, and so forth.

These low-risk self-disclosures may, in some cases, be all that is required for reciprocity satisfaction to be experienced, especially if these disclosures are similar in depth to those made by the speaker (i.e., one's partner). I have found that it is less threatening for some individuals to acquire these self-disclosure behaviors through shaping rather than through direct instruction. Direct instruction may serve only to spotlight the skills deficit and cause defensiveness. Instead, shaping was the strategy chosen for Wade and Louise. An excerpt from a session with the couple that illustrates this shaping process is reproduced below.

Louise: Wade, I'm glad that you decided to continue counseling with me. We have made so much progress in our communications that I'm worried that if we stop coming together we will slip back into our old routine.

Wade: (Nods and smiles but says nothing.)

Therapist: Wade, I noticed that when Louise was speaking you were nodding your head in agreement.

Wade: I was not aware of doing that.

Therapist: Was my interpretation accurate? Do you agree with Louise?

Wade: Yes, I agree we have improved our communications.

Therapist: Louise said that she was worried that you might fall back into the old pattern of relating. How do you feel about that?

Wade: Well, I guess that could happen, and that would not be good. That would be frustrating.

Therapist: I think it would be helpful for Louise, Wade, if you were to let her know when you agree with her and her feelings about things that are important to her.

Wade: I can do that.

Therapist: Wade, can you tell Louise now so that she can hear it from you?

Wade: (To Louise.) I agree with you. We have come a long way in our communications.

Therapist: Very good, Wade. Can you tell Louise how you would feel if you both slipped back into your old pattern of communicating?

Wade: (To Louise.) I would not like that. I guess it would not be good if that happened.

Louise: (To Wade.) I would be sad if that happened again.

Wade: Me, too.

Therapist: (To the couple.) You both agree that going back to the old way of relating would make both of you feel sad. I suggest that, in the future, when you agree with each other, that you express your agreement. It usually brings spouses together when they know they are on the same page.

In teaching Wade affirmative expression and concordance, the emphasis was placed upon Louise's need and not Wade's skills deficit in the area of self-disclosure and reciprocity. Furthermore, at the end of the exchange, both Wade and Louise are asked to continue verbalizing their agreement. Wade is not singled out.

An example of shaping neutral and nondefensive acknowledgment is presented next. The therapy session begins with Wade voicing some concerns.

Wade: (To the therapist.) Dr. B., Louise and I have been having a little problem for the last week or so. We thought that you might be able to help us.

Therapist: What's the nature of the problem?

Wade: Well, it is with one of my employees. He's asked for a raise, but lately his job performance has not been very good. Louise thinks I should let him go and certainly not give him a raise.

Therapist: Why don't you both discuss this issue now. I'll observe and offer suggestions if I think they might be helpful. Wade, why don't you begin.

Wade: OK. (To Louise.) I don't want to fire Michael. He's a good worker, most of the time, but sometimes he just can't seem to get it together.

Louise: I know, but this seems to be happening more lately. He says he has family problems, but his poor performance affects the business.

Wade: I know, sales have been down for the last quarter.

Louise: Yeah, and you've had to pick up the slack. It doesn't seem right, and now he wants a raise. I think he takes advantage of your good nature. He knows how to get to you and that really bothers me.

(Wade is silent. Louise turns to the therapist.)

Louise: Dr. B., I think that Michael is manipulating Wade. I'm really not even sure that he has the family problems he says he has. I think it is just an excuse. I don't think Wade really can see through him. I don't think he understands.

Therapist: (To Wade.) Wade, can you summarize what Louise has said so that she knows you have heard and understood her.

Wade: Yes. (To Louise.) You think Michael is a fraud—some type of con man. You think he takes advantage of my good nature, am I right?

Louise: Yes, that's it in a nutshell.

Wade: Well, I believe in giving people the benefit of the doubt, but no one can manipulate you unless you let them. I don't think Michael is manipulating me. I'll talk to him about his performance. I think I'll offer him an opportunity to work on a commission basis, but there won't be any raise.

Therapist: (To Louise.) What do you think about Wade's solution?

Louise: I guess we should give it a try, but I don't think it will do much good.

Wade: Well, we'll see.

Therapist: I think you both have done very well without much help from me. Wade, it is clear that you really understood Louise's position, even though you don't agree with it. You were able to disagree without being disagreeable. You know, some people think that disagreement gets in the way of being intimate and connected, but that's not so. In true intimacy, there is a healthy respect for differences and separateness. I think that you'll find that when you respect each other's differences, you will feel closer.

Louise: I never looked at it that way. I have always thought that differences of opinion on important matters could lead to divorce.

Therapist: It's not so much the differences that cause problems—it's seeing these differences in terms of right or wrong, good or bad, that causes problems. When different positions are seen in terms of winning or losing—that's when marriages get into serious trouble.

Louise: (Laughs.) Dr. B., you mean to tell me that I'm not always right?

Again, in this example, the focus is not on Wade. When recommendations are offered, they are presented to the couple, not just to one spouse.

It will be recalled that Wade did not have any difficulty disagreeing with Louise. He refused to take on her father's role, and that's what caused the couple to enter treatment. It was the way in which Wade disagreed with Louise that put distance between them. The therapist praised (reinforced) Wade for not being disagreeable. No mention was made of how Wade's style of disagreeing in the past might have been a contributing factor to the couple's difficulties. Emphasizing the positive aspects of a spouse's behavior reduces threats to the self.

Sympathetic sharing sometimes occurs spontaneously. When this happens, the therapist should call attention to it, label it as a significant (reciprocal) self-disclosure, and encourage its continuance. Frequently, it requires the therapist's intervention. This was necessary with Wade and Louise. The following exchanges transpired at the close of one session:

Louise: Dr. B., would it be possible to change our appointment time next week? We won't be able to be here on Tuesday. Either Wednesday or Thursday would be fine.

Therapist: Yes, I believe I have openings. That should not be a problem.

Louise: Thank you. Wade, my mother and I will be going to place flowers on my father's grave. It is the two-year anniversary of his death. (Louise begins to cry.)

Therapist: I'm so sorry for your loss. I think I know how much he meant to you. Both my parents have been dead for years, and I still miss them very much.

Louise: He was a good man. He taught me so much. He was so supportive. He always said that he was so proud of me. I wish he were here. I think you'd like him.

Therapist: He sounds like a great man and a great father. I'm sure I'd like him.

Wade: He was a man of character with a great sense of humor. I admired him. If it weren't for him, Louise and I would never have made it.

Therapist: I know what his backing meant to both of you.

Wade moves closer to Louise on the sofa, takes her hand, and puts his arm around her shoulder. Louise continues to cry.

Therapist: Wade, I can see that you are really moved by Louise's sadness. What effect does her sorrow have upon you?

Wade: I feel so bad for her. I don't know what to do or say. I'm also afraid that she will become depressed again. After her father died, she could not function for awhile. Our internist gave her Prozac. That was a rough time.

Therapist: You're sad and worried at the same time.

Wade: Yes, I don't want her to dwell on it. I'm afraid her depression will only get worse.

Therapist: There is a difference between the normal sadness that comes with mourning and clinical depression. Although, on the surface, they may look the same, they are different. Have you told Louise about your fears?

Wade: Not in so many words, but I think she knows.

Louise: (To Wade.) I didn't know that you were afraid. I thought you thought I was just a big crybaby.

Therapist: (To Wade.) I think it would be helpful to Louise if you talked about your fears and concerns. I think she sees your attempt to protect her as prohibiting her from mourning.

Wade: (To Louise.) Well, like I told Dr. B., I'm afraid of your depression. It makes me sad to see you in pain, and I can't do anything about it.

Therapist: (To Wade.) Ask Louise if there is anything you can do to help.

Wade: (To Louise.) Is there something I can do?

Louise: (To Wade.) Just listen to me. Let me cry it out. That's all.

Therapist: We can't stop people from feeling. No matter how hard we try, the feelings will still be there. For most people, sharing feelings, even negative ones like fear and sadness, can bring a healing closeness.

Louise: (To Wade.) I'd rather hear your fears than hear nothing.

Wade: OK.

DISCUSSION

The presenting problem in this case example was an intrusive mother-in-law. This became the focus of treatment. Boundary creation and maintenance, limit setting, and the realignment of conjugal roles so that Louise could become more competent, effective, and personally responsible in dealing with her mother were all accomplished within a relatively short time. A recalibration in the couple's system had been effected. For all intents and purposes, the presenting problem had been resolved and the treatment contract had been fulfilled. Although it was evident that the presenting problem also served as a defense that protected the spouses and allowed them to avoid dealing with the more central and frightening issues of differing intimacy needs and self-esteem, the focus of treatment remained the presenting problem. Had Louise not proposed additional sessions to deal with her desire for more intimacy with Wade, therapy would have been concluded at this juncture.

SHERRY AND PAUL

The issue that brought this couple in for consultation was Sherry's diminished sexual desire. The couple had been married for about three and a half years. Sherry's loss of sexual interest in Paul had begun about a year before they decided to seek professional assistance.

When the presenting problem is sexual in nature, a Personal Sexual History (Bagarozzi, 2001) is taken in addition to individual, couple, and relational histories in order to determine whether the spouses are appropriate candidates for sex therapy (Weeks & Gambescia, 2002). Based upon these interviews, no contraindications were evident. Neither spouse was seen as having significant psychopathology, both spouses had a positive view of sex and of themselves as sexual people, and both wanted to resolve the problem. Although Sherry had lost her desire for Paul, she still wanted her sexual feelings for him to return. However, during her individual sessions, Sherry disclosed that she loved Paul "like a brother" but was not sexually attracted to him any longer. She said that she had never been as sexually turned on with him as she had been with other men, but that had been acceptable to her, since Paul had so many other admirable qualities. She added that it never occurred to her that she might lose her desire for him completely. Sherry was very forthcoming. She said that she still found other men sexually attractive and incorporated these men and previous lovers into her masturbatory fantasies. She experienced no guilt or shame about these sexual fantasies since she had no intention of acting upon them. She was committed to Paul.

Relevant Personal History

Sherry

Sherry had grown up in a middle-class suburb of a large midwestern city. She was the eldest of three children. She described her parents as loving, caring, and giving church-going people, but family life was "dull." She characterized the town in which they lived as "boring." After high school, she worked for a travel agency and earned a 2-year college degree; then she underwent training to become a flight attendant for a major airline. When her training was completed, she moved to the southeastern city where the airline was headquartered. Life as a flight attendant was far from being dull. She shared residences with other flight attendants, traveled extensively, and dated frequently. However, acquisitions and mergers, changes in the airline industry, reductions in benefits, less-desirable flying schedules, and an uncertain future took much of the glamour and excitement out of her job. After considering her options, Sherry left her position with the airline and became a partner in a travel agency. She met Paul when he came into the agency to purchase airline tickets for a business trip. Although Paul was a very handsome man, Sherry had not been attracted to him for this reason. She had been with good-looking men in the past. What she found so appealing was his gentleness, kindness, and sincerity. When Paul returned from his business trip, he called Sherry and asked her to have dinner with him. She accepted.

Paul

Paul's father was a surgeon. Before her death, his mother had been active in charitable organizations for most of her life. Paul had one older brother, a high-ranking military officer, and Paul himself was a hospital administrator. He had been divorced from his first wife for about a year before he met Sherry. Paul cited incompatibility as the reason for the failure of his first marriage. He suspected that his wife might have been having an affair but had been unable to verify this. The couple separated amicably, and there were no children from this union. Paul said that Sherry had helped him get over the trauma of his divorce.

ASSESSMENT CONSIDERATIONS

Scores on the Dyadic Adjustment Scale were 108 and 106 for Paul and Sherry, respectively. This placed them in the satisfied and adjusted range for this scale. Both perceived their marriage to be voluntary. The only SIDCARB area of concern for both of them was sexual relations. Similarly, perceived-ideal discrepancies of any significance for Images ratings were identified for items concerning the couple's sexual relationship. Disaffection scores for Sherry and Paul were low, and trust was not an issue for either of them.

Hypoactive sexual desire is sometimes symptomatic of a desire discrepancy between spouses. A desire discrepancy exists when the partners' needs for sexual intimacy, orgasm, intercourse, and so on are significantly different. In some instances, unfortunately, these differences may not come to light until the couple has been married for a time. It is important to determine whether one is dealing with diminished or lost sexual desire or a desire discrepancy, since the goals of treatment will differ depending upon the nature of the condition. When used in conjunction with the Personal Sexual History interviews (Bagarozzi, 2001), the Intimacy Needs Questionnaire (Bagarozzi, 1990, 2001) can be very helpful in making this determination.

Although Sherry's need for sexual intimacy (as measured by the Intimacy Needs Questionnaire) was a little stronger than Paul's, the difference was considered not to be significant. Similarly, the desired frequency of sexual contact (on a weekly basis) for Paul and Sherry was roughly the same. Both agreed that two or three times a week had been the norm prior to Sherry's diminished interest. Therefore, a constitutionally based need discrepancy was not thought to be a contributing factor. When the couple entered treatment, sexual involvement of any type had decreased to about once or twice a month.

As is often the case with hypoactive sexual desire, the identified patient reports satisfaction for both receptivity and reciprocity in the area of sexual intimacy in responding to the Intimacy Needs Questionnaire. The identified patient tends to be primarily concerned with how this condition affects his or her spouse and the marriage. During her personal sexual history interview, Sherry offered this distinction when asked to discuss her attitudes and feelings about her sexual relationship with Paul:

> Paul needs sex to feel good about himself. I like sex because it makes me feel good. Sex with Paul was mostly pleasant but rarely fun or exciting. I felt that even his concerns about me having an orgasm were more for him than for me. He is a good man. I love him, and I don't want to hurt him, but I'm just not turned on to him any longer. I wish I were.

Sherry had always considered herself to be a very sexual, sensual person. Sexuality and sensuality were important components of her self-concept. She took pride in the knowledge that men found her sexually attractive and desirable. She knew that Paul found her attractive, but she felt that he lacked passion. In order to protect his self-esteem, she said nothing to him about her desire for and fantasies about other men or her solitary masturbation; but her own self-esteem began to suffer. She felt regret that she had given up fun and excitement in exchange for security, stability, and predictability. Her life with Paul was beginning to resemble life with her parents—dull and boring.

During Paul's personal sexual history interview, he expressed his fear that Sherry would leave him, as had his first wife. He interpreted her waning desire as a prelude to divorce. This had been the case in his first marriage. He said that he was willing to do whatever it took to save their marriage. Paul's perspective and interpretation of his relationship with Sherry was enlightening. He said that when they began to date, Sherry had been very honest about her past relationships with other men. He understood how important it was for her to see herself as desirable, but he thought that some of the men she had dated had taken advantage of her need to be "wanted." He thought that, in some instances, she had left herself open to exploitation. He described some of the men she dated as "rakes." Paul never told Sherry about his feelings, in order to preserve her self-image. These relationships were a thing of the past, and disparaging them would have served no purpose. He considered himself to be different from most of the men Sherry had been with. He treated her with respect, tenderness, and kindness—not as a "sexual object."

DISCUSSION

This case illustrates how the presenting problem may be used as a defense that allows the spouses to avoid dealing with issues that are threatening to them both. Although hypoactive sexual desire is a serious concern, it represents a problem that the couple agrees would be safe for them to tackle. If some mutually acceptable level of sexual involvement could be negotiated, then homeostasis would be regained. As stated earlier in this volume, if voluntary relationships are to continue satisfactorily for a significant time, both spouses must avoid doing or saying things that would violate unverbalized contractual agreements or damage the partners' selves. In Paul and Sherry's case, their agreement proved to be inadequate. Hypoactive sexual desire was the symptom of this failure, a condition that both agreed could be discussed with the therapist.

INTERVENTION

The treatment of hypoactive sexual desire begins with structured sensate focus exercises (Kaplan, 1979; Masters, Johnson, & Kolodny, 1994; Weeks & Gambescia, 2002). The spouse with this condition usually experiences a variety of emotions, the most common being performance anxiety. Guilt, concern for one's partner, sadness, and reactive depression are also common. In response to a spouse's pressure to engage in intercourse, resentment and shame are often felt. Sensate focus exercises are designed to eliminate these negative emotions through systematic desensitization. The emphasis is on feeling pleasurable sensations rather than sexual arousal. This nondemand approach to physical intimacy disrupts the linear, goal-directed expectation that any type of sensual involvement should automatically lead to sexual intercourse and orgasm. Typically, the couple is asked to refrain from having sexual intercourse until the therapist judges that it is appropriate to do so. Although not originally designed to be a strategic restraining technique by Masters and Johnson (1970), the proscription of sexual intercourse may encourage some couples to become sexually active.

The sensate focus program used with Sherry and Paul was divided into three phases:

1. Nongenital pleasuring
2. Genital pleasuring
3. Nondemand sexual intercourse

By the end of the fifth week of the sensate focus program, Sherry and Paul had progressed to the point where nondemand intercourse was successfully achieved. The couple was then seen every other week for 2 months so that their progress could be monitored. At the close of treatment, Paul and Sherry were having sexual intercourse on an average of once every 7 to 10 days.

DISCUSSION

In response to a 6-month follow-up questionnaire mailed to the couple (see Appendix A), Sherry called for an individual appointment. In this interview, she said that she and Paul were having intercourse on a weekly basis and that she was enjoying it more. Sometimes she still had to "psych" herself before becoming sexual with Paul, but added that once she "got in the mood," sex with Paul was "pleasant." At the close of the session, she thanked me and mentioned that she and Paul were now "ready to have a baby." I recommended that she and Paul return for some additional work. She said that she would think about my recommendation.

In this case example, we see how both spouses were very careful and deliberate in their efforts to avoid doing or saying what they believed might be hurtful to each other or damaging to their relationship. Paul believed that Sherry's self-worth was sexually based and that this had made her vulnerable to sexual exploitation in the past. Sherry viewed Paul's need for sex as an affirmation of his competence as a man and not an indication of his genuine desire for her. His tender, caring, respectful approach to their lovemaking was experienced by her as passionless. As a long-term treatment goal, helping the spouses explore the validity of their unverbalized assumptions about each other may have increased understanding and paved the way for a more intimate and satisfying sexual relationship. However, the sensate focus procedure had been effective in increasing the couple's sexual activity and enhancing Sherry's level of desire to some degree. Therefore, this brief behaviorally focused sex therapy had dealt successfully with the presenting problem and restored the couple's homeostatic balance.

When the presenting problem is a collusive defense, it means that the couple is not ready or able to tackle more frightening issues in their relationship. Understanding and respect for the couple's position lays the foundation for therapeutic trust. Successful resolution of the presenting problem will make it easier, should the need arise, for the couple to return for treatment in the future, as I had recommended for Sherry and Paul.

When the presenting problem is thought to represent a collusive defense, the therapist might find it helpful to consider the questions outlined below.

1. What is the problem that the couple presents to the therapist for resolution?
2. What are the underlying issues, conflicts, or difficulties that the presenting problem allows the couple to avoid?
3. What are the unverbalized clauses in this collusive contract that make conflict avoidance possible? What must each partner do (or not do) to fulfill his or her part of the contract?
4. How does this contract protect and validate each partner's self?
5. Why is this collusive agreement no longer functional? How has the contract broken down?

STUDY QUESTIONS

1. In this chapter, three types of low-risk self-disclosure communication skills were subtly taught to Wade and Louise: affirmative expressive concordance, neutral or nondefensive acknowledgment, and sympathetic sharing. Can you think of some additional low-risk forms of communication that the therapist might employ to:
   a. Help increase reciprocity satisfaction for Louise?
   b. Support and validate Wade's feelings of competence?
2. The presenting problem that brought Paul and Sherry into treatment was diminished sexual desire, or "hypoactive sexual desire." This condition was thought to be symptomatic of the couple's collusive and mutually protective avoidance of certain sensitive issues that were central to the maintenance of each spouse's feelings of competence and self-worth. Although the presenting problem was dealt with successfully, the underlying issues were deliberately not addressed by the therapist, who had contracted with the couple for short-term problem-focused behavioral sex therapy. When Sherry met with the therapist in response to a 6-month follow-up inquiry, it was evident that her sexual relationship with her husband was still not very satisfying to her. Sherry's self-initiated visit to the therapist, therefore, was seen as an indirect request for further assistance. However, she showed little interest in returning for additional work with Paul.
   a. Knowing that there are a number of unresolved issues for Sherry in this marriage and that the couple are planning to have a child, is there anything else that the therapist should have said or done?
   b. What are some of the ethical considerations?

Acting Out and Monitoring and Restraining: An Overview 5

This brief chapter focuses on two collusive defensive systems that have received little attention in the clinical literature on marital/family therapy. These couple defenses are both subtle and complex and are usually not identified as problematic by the spouses, since they have become a routine part of the couple's *modus operandi*. These defensive pacts are described below in some detail. Suggestions for identifying these defensive systems and for addressing them therapeutically are offered in Chapter 6.

COLLUSIVE ACTING OUT

The psychoanalytic concept of acting out is used to describe a defensive process that some individuals use to dissipate painful affects, such as anxiety and depression, and to resolve repressed conflicts through current behavioral enactments. Like all defense mechanisms, acting out is not conscious and the person is not aware that his or her behavior is unconsciously driven. Acting out can be thought of as a behavioral substitute for the self-contained neurotic symptom that presents as an overt manifestation of an internal intrapsychic conflict. By acting out, the conflict is externalized. Fenichel (1945) explains that the external environment serves only as an arena within which the person stages and replays intrapsychic conflicts. By acting out, the individual does not have to remember these painful conflicts and the affects associated with them; in this sense, acting out aids repression. Through acting out, the person attempts to gain mastery over past traumatic experiences by actively seeking out or recreating scenarios that are similar to the traumatic ones in the hope that the outcome will be different, that the trauma will be mastered, and the conflict resolved. By acting out, he or she recreates the traumatic event on a smaller scale under controlled circumstances thought to be manageable. Unfortunately, this does not resolve the conflict and only provides temporary relief from the painful affects associated with it.

People and interpersonal situations that are associatively and symbolically connected with these repressed conflicts often serve as unconscious stimuli for their reenactment. As is the case with all transferential phenomena, acting out is usually highly dramatic and emotional. Such histrionic displays can alert the therapist to the possibility that acting out may be taking place.

It has been my clinical experience that acting out can become a strategy that a person uses to deal with unpleasant affects in general, especially when the behavior has been rewarded. For example, I treated a woman who had been traumatized at the age of 9, when her father announced that he was divorcing her mother. In response to this news, she flew into a rage and attacked her father. Later in life she exhibited violent temper outbursts in response to people, events, and situations that she experienced as particularly frustrating. For this woman, temper tantrums had become a characteristic manipulative strategy that enabled her to get her way with her husband, children, relatives, and friends.

Collusive acting out in marriage can take a variety of forms. In its simplest form, a spouse will act out his or her partner's unacceptable and repressed feelings, behaviors, desires, and so on. As is the case with individuals, this process occurs unconsciously and neither spouse is aware of the underlying dynamic. The following example illustrates this point.

> Helena was referred to me by her attorney for "anger management" after she was arrested for assault and battery. The incident that prompted her arrest took place in a local bar. She and her husband, Brad, had met friends for drinks one evening. While she and Brad were waiting their turn to shoot pool, two men who had just entered the bar began to use the pool table. Brad politely informed the men that they would have to wait their turn and that other people were waiting to play. The men ignored Brad and continued their game. Brad asked them again, but they only laughed at him and told him to "get lost." When Brad did not respond, Helena became indignant. She confronted one of the men and grabbed the pool cue from his hand. An argument ensued, and he called Helena a "stupid bitch," among other insulting names. In response to these insults, Helena hit him with the pool cue and the police were called.

At first glance, one might be tempted to see Helena's aggression as a case of poor impulse control and not as an example of collusive acting out, but this was not an isolated incident. An examination of the couple's relationship history brings the collusive dynamic into focus.

One of the traits that first attracted Helena to Brad was his gentle nature. Over the years, however, she believed that his kindness was being exploited by others. Eventually, she became frustrated with what she considered to be Brad's "submissiveness," and she decided that she would take matters into her own hands. She described two incidents that had taken place in the past year. The first occurred when she and Brad had gone out to dinner. Brad was about to pull into a parking space when another driver cut him off and took the spot. Helena became furious when Brad did nothing. He simply drove around for an additional 15 minutes until he was able to find another spot some distance from the restaurant. He complained briefly about the incident to Helena and then dropped the matter. Helena, however, could not let it go. During dinner she excused herself in order to go to the restroom. Instead, she slipped out of the restaurant, went into the parking lot, found the car whose driver had taken their parking place, and threw a rock through the windshield. She returned to the restaurant and said nothing to Brad about what she had done until they were back at home. Brad said that he thought her action was "extreme," but made no further comments.

The second incident took place when Brad's older brother, Charles, came to visit. Brad had been the butt of Charles's sarcastic humor when the two boys were growing up. This pattern continued into adulthood. Brad dreaded Charles's visits but accepted them as an inevitable part of family life. Helena, however, saw Brad's acceptance of Charles's hostility as another example of his "submissiveness." Charles's treatment of Brad on his last visit was the "straw that broke the camel's back." The night before Charles left, Helena told him that he was no longer welcome in their home. When Charles asked Brad if he agreed with Helena's decision, Brad was noncommittal. His response was, "I think we all need to cool down a little." The next morning, Charles left without saying a word.

A key element in collusive acting out is subtlety. Brad could honestly say that he had never encouraged Helena to act out his anger and frustration, and Helena would take full responsibility for her aggressive acts. By not condemning, and thereby reinforcing, Helena's behavior, Brad's self-concept as a good and gentle man was affirmed and Helena's self-concept as a strong and self-sufficient woman was validated.

It is not uncommon to come across relationships in which both spouses act out for each other. This process of reciprocal acting out should be suspected when both spouses have become involved in conflicts with their respective in-laws or other members of the extended family. The following example is a case in point.

Dan was a federal law enforcement officer. At 6 feet 3 inches tall, he was an imposing figure. The relationship among the members of Dan's family of origin is best characterized as being structurally separated. Little emotion was permitted expression in Dan's family, and those emotions that were allowed were restricted in terms of their intensity. Dan's parents were models of stoicism and restraint. Dan's wife, Pam, on the other hand, came from a larger, chaotically enmeshed extended family system. Emotions, as well as unsolicited opinions and advice, were freely expressed by all family members. When Dan was promoted to a senior-level position, his parents and siblings congratulated him in their usual understated way—firm handshakes from his father and brothers, and measured hugs from his mother and sister. Pam, however, was ecstatic. She expressed the joy, excitement, and pride that Dan was unable to experience. Such expressions would be frowned upon by Dan's family. Pam acted them out for him. Pam became Dan's safety valve.

Pam's difficulties with her mother began shortly after the birth of her first child. She was critical of Pam's mothering, telephoned her daily to offer advice, and would visit Pam unexpectedly, since she lived only a few miles away.

Pam was not consciously aware of how disturbing her mother's intrusions had become, but Dan noticed the change in her behavior, especially after one of her mother's unanticipated visits. Pam was becoming increasingly depressed and irritable. In enmeshed relationships in which separation and individuation are incomplete, personal ego boundaries are usually blurred and permeable, systems boundaries are porous, feelings tend to interfere with thinking, and judgments become impaired. Gradually, Pam started to doubt her own competence as a mother. This was not a case of Pam's inability to maintain systems boundaries that had already been established or to define personal boundaries between herself and her mother. The problem was that in Pam's extended family, such boundaries were virtually nonexistent. In Pam's family, everyone knew everyone else's business. Even a couple's most intimate details were shared with other family members without reservation.

As Pam's condition worsened, Dan stepped in. He told Pam's mother that she was to discontinue unannounced visits and that she should refrain from offering unsolicited advice about Pam's parenting. Pam's parents were offended by Dan's admonitions, which they shared with the extended family, but no one was willing to confront "Mr. Law and Order."

Dan had no difficulty whatsoever with Pam's family labeling him as an insensitive and rigid person, since the net result was a sharp reduction in Pam's mother's invasiveness. Pam's parents considered Dan to be the problem, and this allowed Pam to maintain a positive but less enmeshed relationship with them.

On the surface, the reciprocal acting out engaged in by this couple may not appear to be a cause for concern, but this defensive process impedes the development of the self. The differentiation of feelings and their expression may never develop for Dan, and he may continue to lead an emotionally barren life. The outcome for Pam may be that she will be unable to complete the process of separation-individuation.

As a general rule, when a spouse acts out for his or her partner, the therapist should consider the possibility that the other spouse is reciprocating. The therapist should always keep in mind that when acting out is part of a couple's defensive system, it may be used against the therapist whenever threats to the self and/or the system are perceived. This can manifest itself in negative provocations by one spouse. When reciprocal acting out occurs in therapy, however, the therapist may experience only the acting out that is directed at him or her, while the reciprocal aspect of the process goes undetected.

COLLUSIVE MONITORING AND RESTRAINING

The opposite side of collusive acting out is collusive monitoring and restraining. This term is used to describe the cybernetic process in which one spouse or partner acts as a regulatory control device whose function is to supervise and keep in check his or her mate's undesirable, inappropriate, problematic, potentially dangerous, unacceptable behavior, and so on. Such overinvolvement and enmeshment is not easily recognized and may come to light only when it fails. Essentially, in collusive monitoring and restraining, one spouse or partner takes the major responsibility for the compensatory functioning of his or her partner's defective ego performances and/or superego failings. Monitoring and restraining can be seen in many areas of ego functioning, such as reality testing and the regulation of drives and impulses. All aspects of superego functioning are also subject to this process (e.g., praise and protection, criticism, and punishment).

It may be difficult to distinguish the various types of acting out from problems with drive regulation and impulse control. Personal histories can be very helpful in this regard, since chronic impulse-control and conduct disorders that first appear in childhood and continue into adult life are more likely to be symptomatic of defective ego functioning and less indicative of acting out. However, it would not be unusual for a repressed individual to choose a spouse with impulse-control problems who would act out his or her unconscious wishes and desires. A distinguishing factor is usually the other spouse's response to the partner's problematic behavior. In collusive acting out, the other spouse is not usually disturbed by his or her mate's actions. In monitoring and restraining, on the other hand, the other spouse is truly upset and strives to control, manage, curtail, or rectify the behavior and feels personally responsible for the other's transgressions. Eventually, the other spouse becomes frustrated and fatigued and decides that he or she can no longer continue along this path—the homeostatic limits have been exceeded and the unspoken contract has been broken. It is at this point that the frustrated spouse will most likely initiate therapy.

Often, during the beginning stages of relationship development, monitoring and restraining may be seen by both spouses as manifestations of love and caring. Later on, however, the monitoring and restraining spouse begins to feel burdened and the monitored spouse begins to feel controlled and confined.

Unlike collusive acting out, collusive monitoring and restraining are conscious processes. Negative feedback and punishment are the corrective measures most commonly used after a problem occurs or a transgression has taken place. To avoid possible difficulties when judgment, insight, and other executive ego functions are required, some couples manage to preplan behavioral responses before entering situations that have proven to be problematic for a spouse in the past. While this feedforward strategy may be successful in heading off potential difficulties, it still requires the oversight, involvement, and cooperation of both partners. Monitoring and restraining are the central thematic dynamics and driving forces in relationships where alcoholism, substance abuse, infidelity, and other issues are involved.

The payoff for the apparently overfunctioning monitoring and restraining spouse is a false sense of mastery and control. This is especially true when monitoring and restraining are also used to prevent one's spouse from acting out one's unconscious motives, wishes, desires, and impulses. Externalization and projective identification are important components in this process.

In therapy, the monitoring and restraining partner presents as the responsible one. He or she is the one who sees to it that appointments are kept, homework assignments are completed, bills are paid promptly, checks don't bounce, and so on. The countertransferential pull would be to align with this spouse or take over that spouse's role as monitor and restrainer. It is important not to lose sight of the fact that deviation amplification and overcorrection have caused the couple system to go into crisis. What couples want the therapist to do is help them regain their previously existing equilibrium and recalibrate their system slightly so that they will still be able to use their characteristic defenses more efficiently. When working with acting out or monitoring and restraining, as with all collusive defenses, the therapist should ask himself or herself the two questions in the following section. Although the answers to these questions may be purely speculative, posing them will help the therapist to consider the possible ramifications of his or her interventional endeavors before they are implemented.

STUDY QUESTIONS

1. What might happen to this marriage/relationship if the couple's collusive defenses were dismantled and removed?
2. Can I help this couple replace their defenses with a different structure and mode of functioning? That is, would it be possible to help them achieve a more rewarding relationship that would also contribute to the development of each spouse and the system as a whole?

Acting Out: Case Examples and Treatment 6

GEORGE AND PENNY

Diana had sought treatment for depression after her husband's untimely death from a stroke when he was in his early fifties. Treatment was successful and therapy was concluded after 10 months. Two years later I received a call from her son, George, who requested that I meet with him to discuss a serious problem that had developed between his wife, Penny, and Diana. He said that the problem was "too complicated" to discuss over the phone and he preferred to talk with me in person. We arranged an appointment for later in the week.

When George arrived at my office he was casually dressed. He had brought two containers of Starbucks coffee and offered me one. He said that his mother had mentioned that I was a coffee drinker so he took the liberty of buying a cup for me. I thanked him and asked about Diana. He said she was not doing well and hoped that I would be able to help. I asked him to tell me about the problem.

George related a series of events that had culminated in a heated confrontation between his wife, Penny, and his mother. About a year after Diana ended her treatment with me, she began to date Sam, with whom she had been casually acquainted through mutual friends for many years and who had recently been divorced. Penny became suspicious about their relationship and asked George if he thought that Diana had been having an affair with Sam while he was still married. George said that he did not think his mother would do such a thing and the matter was closed as far as George was concerned; but not for Penny, who decided to conduct her own "investigation." She contacted Sam's ex-wife to ask if she, too, had similar suspicions and received confirmation that she did, although she had no concrete evidence to substantiate them. When Diana found out about Penny's investigation, she confronted her, and their relationship began to deteriorate. Penny did not believe Diana's denials and was convinced that the couple had been having an affair. She then decided not to allow her children to visit their grandmother when Sam was present in Diana's home.

When I asked George how he felt about Penny's decision, he said that there wasn't much he could do about it. In response to my next question about how he thought I might be able to help, he said that perhaps I could "talk some sense into Penny." After stating that I could not take sides in the family's conflicts, I offered to meet with him, Penny, and Diana to attempt a resolution of the conflict. George said he would have to talk with Penny to see if she would be agreeable.

George called about 3 weeks later and related that Penny did not want to meet with Diana—that there was "nothing to talk about." After telling George that I understood how stressful this situation was for them, I offered to meet with him and Penny as an alternative. He agreed to propose this to Penny, but did not think she would be interested. After another few weeks went by, George called again. He said that circumstances had changed and Penny had agreed to meet with me.

When George and Penny came in, Penny said that she knew I had treated Diana for depression and had a relationship with her, but that she, Penny, wanted to tell her "side of the story." I assured Penny that I had not talked with Diana about the situation, had spoken only with George, and was glad that she had decided to meet with me to present her side of the story.

Penny: We never liked Sam. Even when Stephen, George's father, was alive, we didn't like him.

Therapist: Penny, when you say "we," what people are you referring to?

Penny: George, for one, and his sister, and me.

Therapist: George, what are your thoughts and feelings about what Penny just said?

George: She's right. He was not our favorite person, but he was sometimes included in my parents' circle of friends, so we tolerated him.

Therapist: What is it about Sam that you don't like?

Penny: He's a sleazy snake in the grass. I know he always had his eye on Diana even when Stephen was alive. When he died, Sam moved right in. He pretended that he was comforting Diana, but he had other intentions.

Therapist: George, what is your take on this?

George: He did spend a lot of time at Mom's house after my father died.

Therapist: How did you feel about that?

George: At first I didn't think about it much, but even after Mom was no longer depressed, he kept showing up.

Therapist: How did that make you feel?

George: I felt uncomfortable in my parents' house—the house I grew up in.
Penny: George, you know you didn't like it.
George: Mom was pretty vulnerable at that time. That was before she came to see you, and she leaned on Sam. I think he took advantage of her.
Penny: But she could have stopped it. George, you know she encouraged it.
George: Well, I'm not so sure about that.
Penny: She did, and you know it, and now they are talking about getting married. Don't pretend you like the idea.
George: Well, there is nothing I can do about it.
Penny: But I won't be part of it, and I won't let the children be part of it, either.
George: You see, Dr. B., this is the problem. Penny says she won't let our children attend their wedding. She says once they marry, she won't even let the children visit them.
Penny: Dr. B., can you blame me? They are setting such a bad example.
George: The children love Diana. It's not right to cut them off from her. They don't understand, but they have asked why Mr. Sam doesn't come to Diana's house anymore when they are there.
Therapist: Penny, how would you like this situation to turn out? What alternatives are acceptable to you?
Penny: She could not marry that slime ball, but that still won't change my opinion of him.
George: That's not realistic. That's not happening.
Therapist: George, do you have any suggestions? Do you see any way out of this dilemma?
George: I don't know. I need to think about it for awhile. Maybe we need to talk about it a little more. We need to take the kids into consideration. We need to see the big picture.
Therapist: Penny, what are your thoughts?
Penny: Let me think about it a little. George will call you if we decide to come back.

DISCUSSION

Prior to my meeting with George and Penny, the problem was presented as a classic mother-in-law/daughter-in-law conflict where a husband is caught between his mother and his wife. However, it did not take long to suspect that Penny was acting out George's anger toward his mother and Sam. This does not mean that Penny herself was not angry about something. Her strong and intense emotional reaction and her disproportionate and absolutist response toward the situation was telling. George's role in this collusive pact was well concealed.

Although I did not have the opportunity to conduct individual sessions with George and Penny, where personal and relationship histories could be gathered, I had learned a considerable amount about George's personal development and his relationship with Penny from the work I had done with Diana. This information made it a little easier to identify the collusive acting-out dynamic.

Relevant Historical Data

George had been an outstanding athlete in high school, who lettered in three sports. In college, he played baseball during his freshman year but did not return to the team for his sophomore year, in order to devote more time to his studies. Although his coaches and friends urged him to continue, George chose the strict academic route. During the fall of his second year, when he was 18 years old, he met Penny, a 22-year-old senior. They shared the same circle of friends but did not date. After Penny graduated, she and George would see each other occasionally at parties, concerts, social gatherings, and so on. When George graduated, he and Penny began to date exclusively. When they married, George was 24 and Penny 28. They had their first child 2 years later, and a second child 18 months after that.

Penny's parents were no longer living when she and George married. She had two older brothers who lived abroad. George and Penny lived only minutes from his parents and they visited often. Visits became even more frequent after Stephen's death. George began to take on many of the household maintenance duties that his father had once performed. Everyone seemed satisfied with this arrangement until Diana began to date Sam. Little by little, Sam began to assume these responsibilities. This angered George, but he said nothing to either Penny or Diane. However, he did complain about Sam's intrusiveness in a telephone conversation with his sister that Penny overheard. As mentioned earlier, subtlety is a key element in acting out. If George had not wanted his wife to know about his true feelings, he would have made sure that she was out of earshot when he voiced his concerns to his sister.

Further Developments

A few days after I met with George and Penny, Diana phoned to request that we schedule a session. She said that she knew I could not discuss my meeting with Penny and George but that she just needed to talk to someone she trusted. We made an appointment to meet. She began:

Diana: Dr. Bagarozzi, I don't know what to do. My family is coming apart.
Therapist: I know. I am truly sorry for what you are going through. How can I help you?
Diana: I don't know if there is anything you can do. I just need someone to talk to. I asked Penny and George if they would come with me to meet with you, but she said she did not want to come.

Therapist: So, you and Penny are still on speaking terms. That's a good sign.

Diana: It's superficial. We talk about the kids, but I don't see them as much as I used to and it's breaking my heart.

Therapist: My wife and I have four grandsons. I could not imagine what it would be like for us if we were not able to see them frequently, so I know something about how you must feel.

Diana: And it will get even worse once Sam and I are married. Penny has made it clear that she doesn't want her children involved with Sam.

Therapist: This is a very unhappy situation for everyone involved. I—

Diana: (Interrupts.) Dr. Bagarozzi, you know me very well. I swear to you that I did not have an affair with Sam while he was married. We were friends. I knew he was having trouble with his wife. They had been having problems for years, but I would never come between a husband and wife.

Therapist: Diana, I do know you pretty well, I think, and I don't believe that you would act against your moral convictions.

Diana began to sob. I handed her a box of tissues and waited silently until she gained her composure. She used the remaining time to fill me in on what had been happening in her life since we last spoke, and talked about her relationship with Sam. Before she left, I said that I would be available to meet with her, her family, and Sam to see if some type of resolution could be reached. Diana commented that she was not very hopeful and that it was in "God's hands."

THEORETICAL CONSIDERATIONS

Acting out is an overt manifestation of an unconscious contractual agreement between spouses that is used to protect both partners and maintain dyadic stability. It is usually easier to understand how the behavior of the acting-out spouse protects his or her mate, but it is more difficult to discover how this dynamic also benefits the acting-out spouse, since that partner is usually not seen in a very positive light. This task is made more difficult when personal histories are sketchy or not available, but sometimes that is all we have at our disposal. Helping George resolve his difficulties with his mother and Sam would deal with only one part of the equation. Penny must also be included if lasting change were to be expected.

Several weeks after my session with Diana, George called again. He said that his mother and Sam had set a wedding date and that his relationship with Penny was growing progressively worse. He added that his children were beginning to show signs of stress and wanted to know why they were not visiting their grandmother as frequently as they had in the past. We set up an appointment for him and Penny.

When George and Penny arrived, they were both angry and immediately began to argue. I suggested that our meeting might be more productive if they could learn to use some communication skills. Penny said that communication was not their problem, "Diana and Sam are our problem." I asked her if she had any idea how their problem could be solved.

Penny: Well, it looks like she is going to marry the bastard, and there is nothing we can do about that.

Therapist: George, what are your feelings about your mother marrying Sam?

George: I don't like it. It is very frustrating.

Therapist: I think Penny is expressing the anger and frustration you both feel about this marriage. Sometimes couples do that. One person is more vocal and the other is silent for the most part. I'm curious. Does this happen in any other areas of your relationship?

Penny: With the boys. When he gets mad at them, I'm the one who has to punish them. I'm the heavy.

Therapist: Penny, are there any other areas in your relationship where you express feelings for George or act for him?

Penny: Not that I can think of. He certainly lets me know when he wants to have sex. He has no trouble expressing those feelings and acting on them.

Therapist: It sounds like the problem has to do with negative feelings, like anger and frustration.

Penny: You could say that. George always has to be the nice guy. Everyone likes George. I'm the bitch, especially now.

Therapist: George, I know it won't change things, but if you spoke with Diana about your misgivings, then Penny would not have to speak for you. She would not have to be the bitch.

Penny: I don't mind being the bitch if it saves my family.

Therapist: Saves them from what?

Penny: We spend too much time with Diana. There is hardly any time for us as a family to do things together.

George: That never seemed to bother you before.

Penny: It's different now. It was OK before we were married and before we had the boys. We have to have a family of our own.

George: We do. You're making a mountain out of a molehill.

Penny: No, I'm not. We go to Diana's a lot, and you go by yourself at least once a week to see her after work.

George: That's only since my father died and my sister moved away after she got married.

Therapist: George, this sounds like a complicated situation. You feel responsible for your mother but angry with her for planning to marry Sam.

George: No, I don't feel responsible for her. She was lonely after Dad died. You know how hard she took it.

Therapist: Yes, I do.

George: I hated to see her like that. After a while we urged her to date, to go out and meet new people, but she wouldn't. You know how long it took her to get rid of my father's belongings.

Therapist: Yes, I remember. That was difficult for her.

George: So, it is not like I don't want her to remarry and have a good life. It's just Sam. There is something weird about having him around.

Penny: It's sick if you ask me. I think we should just let them be. Let them have their own life. We don't have to be involved.

George: We can't just pretend they don't exist. She's my mother and the kids love her.

Therapist: Penny, is there some kind of compromise? Some sort of middle ground?

Penny: George can take the boys to visit their grandmother from time to time. Maybe once a month or so, but I'll stay home. I won't go. She can come here to visit without Sam. I won't have that man in my home.

George: What about the wedding?

Penny: What about it? I told you I won't go.

George: I'm taking the boys. I will not spoil my mother's wedding, and I will not prevent my children from being with their grandmother on such an important day. That's cruel. The whole family will be there. Our friends will be there. Their cousins will be there. They will not understand. I will take them. That's for sure.

Penny: Whatever.

The session ended on that note, and I had no further contact with George and Penny. At Christmas, Diana and Sam sent me a greeting card. Diana had enclosed a short letter. She and Sam had been married for almost 6 months and were doing relatively well, under the circumstances. She was not able to see her grandchildren as often as she would have preferred, and her personal contacts with George had decreased considerably, although he telephoned her frequently. She thanked me for my help and said that she and George had a "really good conversation" after one of my sessions with him and Penny. She said that George told her about his anger and his disappointment in her for marrying Sam. Although this was hard for her to hear, she appreciated his honesty. She described her relationship with Penny as "cool." Penny's visits were rare and of short duration. Penny was cordial to Sam but did not interact with him very much at family gatherings. Diana saw this as a "slight improvement" but she did not have any "great expectations." She was puzzled by what appeared to be an improvement in George and Penny's relationship.

PROCESS ANALYSIS

Once acting out is interpreted to a couple as a dynamic, it can no longer be ignored. This does not mean that the process will be discontinued, but it can no longer remain an unconscious collusive one. It is important to remember that acting out has a counterpart. It represents only one spouse's contribution to the quid pro quo contractual agreement that is there to protect the self and maintain the system. It is often difficult to know how the acting-out spouse benefits from the problematic behavior, since, in many instances, the payoff may not come about for some time and is usually not apparent to the outside observer. At first, I was inclined to see Penny's escalating behavior as a deviation-amplifying overcorrection that had gotten out of control, but then she made the comment about saving her family. The remarks that followed this statement made it clear what purpose acting out served for her. Penny was also using this behavior to protect her children from Diana's influence, to bring about a separation between George and his family of origin, and to erect definable boundaries between the two families. Acting out was seen as a drastic attempt to bring about a critical developmental transition.

Standard pretreatment assessment procedures were not used in this case. To ask George and Penny to undergo such an assessment would have been countertherapeutic and inappropriate, given the crisis nature of the presenting problem, and probably would have driven Penny away. Without detailed personal histories, however, the transferential components of the acting-out scenario remained unknown. Subsequently, I learned from George's sister, who had returned to the area and entered treatment to deal with the aftermath of a difficult divorce, that Penny's father had been unfaithful to her mother.

Acting out is a symptom; like most symptoms, it is a symbolic representation of an underlying complex of related conflicts. Just as dream symbols can never be fully interpreted, symptoms are never fully explained or understood, since they are multidetermined. Clearly, the issue of infidelity was not resolved for Penny, and one cannot know how this conflict might manifest itself in the future. Similarly, one cannot assume that acting out as one of this couple's collusive defenses was completely abandoned by George and Penny. Finally, one cannot know what aspects of the couple's selves were being preserved and protected by the continued use of this defensive operation.

PHIL AND TERRY

Phil and Terry were engaged to be married but had not set a wedding date. They had been living together for about 18 months, but periodic conflicts caused them to question their compatibility as a couple. Terry contacted me to inquire about "premarital counseling." She had been referred to me by a couple who had gone through the Premarital Education and Training Sequence Program (PETS)

(Bagarozzi & Bagarozzi, 1982; Bagarozzi, Bagarozzi, Anderson, & Pollane, 1984) some years earlier. I scheduled an appointment for her and Phil for the following week.

Premarital Educational and Training Sequence: An Overview

The PETS model is a content-specific educational and skills training program. The first few sessions are devoted to skills acquisition. Functional communication, conflict negotiation, and problem-solving skills are taught. When these skills have been mastered, the couple receive a program packet containing the following instruments, which they are asked to complete:

1. Images (a 35-item assessment questionnaire)
2. The Intimacy Needs Questionnaire
3. The Trust Scale

The content portion of the packet targets nine critical areas of marriage:

1. Marital roles, tasks, duties, responsibilities, and expectations
2. Financial management and financial decision making
3. Religion, spirituality, and values
4. Sexual relations
5. Children, parenthood, and child-rearing practices
6. In-law relationships, immediate family, and extended family involvement
7. Friendships
8. Social and recreational involvements and expectations
9. Relationships, obligations, responsibilities, involvements, expectations, and so on with former spouses, in-laws, and children from previous marriages

For each content area, each member of the couple is asked to consider a series of issue that often cause conflicts between partners. Using the communication, conflict negotiation, and problem-solving skills that they have acquired, the partners are asked to resolve any disagreements or differences of opinion that these issues pose for them. The couple is directed to record, in writing, agreed-upon solutions. If they are unable to reach an agreement about a particular issue, that issue is temporarily set aside. Once all content areas have been dealt with, those issues that have not been satisfactorily resolved are revisited, at which time the couple are asked to attempt to resolve them a second time. Any issues that the couple cannot resolve after the second attempt are again tabled.

Next, the couple are asked to repeat this process to resolve any problems that were identified through the use of the assessment instruments. At the conclusion of this exercise, only those issues and problems that the couple have been unable to resolve remain. The potential spouses are then asked to evaluate how important a satisfactory resolution of these issues and problems is considered to be for the future success of their marriage.

The PETS Contract

Couples who choose to participate in PETS understand that the program is intended to provide education and skills training—that it is not a therapeutic one designed to treat serious relationship problems. Couples are informed that if major conflicts arise that they are unable to resolve using the skills they have acquired, they might consider a more therapeutic format once they have completed PETS. Since program's goals can be met in a relatively short time (i.e., 8 to 10 sessions), detailed personal and relationship histories are not gathered, as is customary with couples who present for marital therapy. However, a history of the couple's relationship is taken during the couple's initial interview.

Relevant Background Information

Phil was 35 years old and Terry 29 when they met. Phil had been divorced from his first wife for several years before he and Terry began to date. Although never married, Terry had been engaged to a man who was killed in an automobile accident shortly before the couple's scheduled wedding. Terry and Phil dated for approximately a year before they decided to live together.

Phil's parents divorced when he was 4. After their divorce, his father moved away and Phil had little contact with him. When he was a teenager, his mother remarried. Phil described his stepfather as a quiet man whom his mother dominated. At 18, Phil joined the navy. After his military service, he attended college. He married his first wife when he was 27. That marriage lasted for 5 years before she divorced him. They had no children.

Terry's father died when she was 15. Her older brother had moved out of the parental home a few years before their father's death. Her mother remarried when Terry was a freshman in college. Shortly after graduating, Terry met her future fiancé. They dated for several years prior to their engagement. After her fiancé's death, Terry dated casually until she met Phil.

Phil and Terry's Progress Through the PETS Program

Phil and Terry were asked to rank order, from least problematic to most problematic, the nine content areas prior to beginning the problem-solving and conflict negotiation process. Beginning with content areas that are easy to resolve provides the couple with immediate reinforcement and gives them an incentive to go on to deal with those content areas that are more challenging. Content area nine was considered by the couple not to be relevant and it was, therefore, not included in the hierarchy. Since Phil and Terry had been living together for more than a year and a half, it did not take them very long to work through most of the content areas satisfactorily. Only two content areas posed serious problems for them: (5) children, parenthood, and child rearing; and (6) in-law/immediate family relationships and extended family involvement.

Even though content area 5 was ranked as less problematic than was content area 6, Phil and Terry agreed that resolving a number of issues between Terry and her mother and stepfather should be addressed before any discussions about children, parenthood, and so forth could take place. In the seventh session, the following exchange took place:

Therapist: Phil, can you tell me what concerns you about Terry's relationship with her parents?

Phil: Her mother is abusive. She has been abusive all her life. I told Terry that if we decide to have children, I will not allow her mother to treat them the way she treats Terry.

Therapist: Terry, what are your thoughts and feelings about Phil's comments?

Terry: Phil is right. My mother can be very abusive, verbally abusive, mostly. She has never been physically abusive, but she can be verbally and emotionally abusive. Still is.

Therapist: Terry, how does she behave when she is abusive?

Terry: She screams. She cusses. She tells me that I'm worthless—that I am an ungrateful daughter. She won't talk to me. When I was little, she'd ignore me for days—sometimes weeks. It was like I wasn't there. I was frightened a lot of the time.

Phil: And her stepfather did nothing. He just let it all happen.

Terry: I never knew what to expect from her. Sometimes she was nice and kind, and then she would turn on me. It was like walking around on eggshells. I got out of there as soon as I could.

Phil: Doc, I don't know why she is still involved with her mother. The woman is evil.

Terry: Dr. B., my mom is mentally ill. She has had two nervous breakdowns and had to be put in a hospital. I understand her now, but as a child I did not.

Phil: But she still hurts and upsets you. Last week after you got off the phone with her, you got sick. You threw up. You couldn't eat. You could not get to sleep.

Terry: (Crying.) He's right.

Phil: Doc, I called her up and read her the riot act. I told her that she could not treat Terry that way, and she called me an asshole. Told me to mind my own business. Then she hung up. I called her back, but she would not answer the phone. She has caller I.D., and knew it was me.

Therapist: I understand your desire to protect Terry.

Phil: (Raising his voice.) I have to. She won't stand up for herself. I can't just stand there and let it happen, like her stepfather does. I get so mad at her when she lets her mother do that to her.

Terry: Dr. B., when Phil gets like this, there is no reasoning with him. I shut down. I don't want to be around him.

Therapist: I wonder if his behavior brings back memories of your childhood experiences with your mother?

Terry: In some ways it does, but Phil is not abusive. He has never been abusive in any way, but when he gets mad it does scare me. In that way, it's the same, I guess.

Phil: Terry, I don't mean to scare you. I'm just so frustrated with this situation. Doc, this is the only problem we have. I won't let her mother kill our chance to be happy. I don't think she wants Terry to be happy. I truly believe that. Her mother's behavior has gotten worse since we got engaged.

Terry: I think Phil is right. I think my mother is jealous of our relationship. I think she'd be happy if Phil and I split up.

Therapist: You must be pretty angry knowing that.

Terry: More sad than angry.

Therapist: Perhaps Phil expresses the anger for both of you.

Terry: But it does not make things better. It only makes things worse between my mother and me.

Therapist: Terry, what have you done in the past to deal with this problem? What worked? What doesn't work?

Terry: We don't visit them as much, but when we do, I usually hear what a bad daughter I am for not visiting. The same thing happens if I don't call her as much as she thinks I should. She'll call me and tell me that I don't care about her. She'll call me ungrateful. That's her favorite word. I'm an ungrateful daughter.

Therapist: So, less frequent contacts have not been too successful?

Terry: Not really.

Therapist: And Phil standing up for you only makes things worse?

Terry: Yes, most definitely. And there is another thing. There are some relatives she doesn't talk to. If she finds out that I've spoken to them, she attacks me. She thinks I'm talking about her. I'll get a call from her—sometimes late at night—and she'll say something like: "I hear you talked to your Aunt Betty about me!" Then she'll accuse me of being two-faced. There is no way I can defend myself against something like that.

Phil: She is a bully. She takes advantage of your weaknesses. You can't let a bully get away with stuff like that. It only encourages them.

Therapist: Phil, it sounds like you've had some experiences with bullies.

Phil:	Yes, I've had some experience with them growing up in Chicago. One guy went after my cousin. When I was finished with him, his bullying days were over.
Therapist:	So it's hard for you to watch what happens with Terry's mom. You want to protect her from a bully.
Phil:	Damn straight!
Therapist:	But you can't, and that is frustrating.
Phil:	Frustrating is putting it mildly. She should just cut off all contact with her.
Terry:	I can't do that. She is my mother. I just can't do that.
Phil:	Doc, what do you suggest? Can you help us?
Terry:	Dr. Bagarozzi, have you come across this kind of problem before?
Therapist:	Yes. It's not uncommon.
Terry:	Do you think you can help?
Therapist:	I can help you explore some possible strategies for dealing with this situation, but we'll have to put our premarital work on the back burner for awhile.
Terry:	I know. I understand.
Phil:	That's fine with me.

DISCUSSION

Transferential and countertransferential dynamics are often a part of collusive acting out. Both were clearly evident in Phil and Terry's relationship and had to be taken into account in devising treatment strategies for the couple. It has been my experience to find that the dyadic stabilizing functions that acting out provides are usually not sustainable for extended periods of time. Eventually the acting-out spouse and his or her target become involved in an escalating cycle, usually culminating in some type of major confrontation that negatively impacts the couple's relationship. Behavior that once brought the spouses together now drives them apart, and whatever self-preserving functions acting out served are overshadowed by the pain, unhappiness, and consternation resulting from the inevitable rift that develops between the two systems. However, I have come across cases where collusive acting out has become a characteristic intergenerational dynamic that does not spiral out of control. In such cases, acting out can be understood as a symptom of an unverbalized contract, the purpose of which is to preserve a precarious balance between the couple system and the parental/family system, of which the target person is only a representative. Reconciling the two systems requires an intergenerational recalibration. One must not lose sight of the fact that collusive acting out, like any symptom, permits the spouses to avoid dealing with major conflicts that exist in their own relationship. Resolving these conflicts by helping couples negotiate more satisfying and equitable relationship contracts is the crux of treatment.

The conflict between Phil and Terry's mother was not seen as symptomatic of a characteristic intergenerational homeostatic compromise. It was viewed as a dyadic stabilizing contractual argument that was no longer viable. Interventions were designed with this in mind. The next session was devoted to helping the couple define the problem in a way that would lend itself to specific behavioral solutions.

Therapist: Now that you have had some time to think about this very touchy situation, I wonder if you have any ideas as to how you both would like your relationship with Terry's mother to be. What do you think would be a realistic and achievable goal?

Terry: I know we can never have a normal mother/daughter relationship. She has been like this ever since I can remember. She is 58 now. She can't change.

Phil: The less we have to do with her, the better off we will be.

Terry: We do have to see them from time to time, and I have to talk to her on the phone every so often, especially when she calls me.

Therapist: Terry, how often do you see your mother?

Terry: About once a month or so. She lives two hours away.

Therapist: How do you feel about the frequency of your visits with her?

Terry: It's not so much the frequency but what happens sometimes when I'm there that is the problem. I get trapped in these arguments with her, and I can't seem to escape.

Therapist: How have you dealt with this situation in the past?

Terry: Well, when Phil is with me, he just steps in and says that it is time to leave, and we leave. I rarely visit her by myself any more. I dread going over there. After this last blowup with Phil, my mother said she doesn't want him to come to her house anymore.

Therapist: How frequently do you talk to her on the telephone?

Terry: Once, maybe two times a week.

Therapist: Do you find yourself being trapped in arguments when you speak on the phone?

Terry: Not as much, but she still can push my buttons over the telephone. She is very difficult to talk to. She is unpredictable. We have caller I.D. Sometimes when she calls, we just don't answer. Sometimes Phil answers and tells her I'm not home. Now, when she hears Phil's voice, she hangs up and won't speak to him.

Therapist: This really sounds like a terrible situation—one that is very upsetting for both of you. I agree with you, Terry. Your mother seems to be very set in her ways, and the chances of her changing are probably very slim. It sounds to me like a relationship management problem.

Terry: What do you mean?

Therapist: You may not be able to change your mother, but you can learn how to structure your interactions with her so that they are less stressful.

Terry: How do I do that?

Therapist: Our environment influences our behavior, to a large degree. Even the most extroverted or hyperactive person will sit quietly in church for the duration of the service. We behave very differently at dinner parties than we do at football games. Our behavior is quite different at a nightclub than it is at a funeral. I suspect that your mother treats you differently when you are in public and when you are around strangers than when you two are alone.

Terry: Yes, she is less aggressive, and she does not put me down as much.

Therapist: Limiting the amount of time you spend together is another effective management technique, and structuring how that time together is spent is also important.

Terry: I try not to spend too much time with her, but sometimes I just can't get away.

Therapist: When does that happen?

Terry: Mostly, when I'm at her house.

Therapist: It sounds like environmental programming, what behaviorists call stimulus control, will prove to be very helpful.

Terry: I hope so, but I'll need your help.

Therapist: We can work on that. There is another strategy that you might consider using.

Terry: What is that?

Therapist: There are ways of communicating that can be used to avert conflict and to de-escalate conflict once it begins. These tactics are a little tricky to learn and take some practice, but they can come in handy in situations where you feel trapped and can't get away as quickly as you would like to. That is something we can look at if you think it would be appropriate.

Terry: I'd like to at least give them a try.

Therapist: Fine. We can begin our planning next week.

Terry: OK.

Phil: It sounds interesting.

INTERVENTION

Transferential and countertransferential dynamics are usually not interpreted or spotlighted for discussion when they surface in therapy. They are noted incidentally, but they do not become the focus of treatment unless they constitute impediments to the couple's progress. In Phil and Terry's case, both dynamics were evident, but they were not determined to be central to the couple's collusive acting out; therefore, they did not become a treatment issue. Even though collusive acting out was the primary concern with Phil and Terry, its role in the couple's defensive repertoire was not addressed directly. It was simply labeled as the couple's unique way of dealing with unpleasant and upsetting emotions such as frustration, anxiety, fear, and anger. Disarming this defense was done subtly and indirectly.

The first task was to ease Phil out of the triangulated acting-out role that he occupied between Terry and her mother. In this case, I did not explicitly say that Terry would be the person primarily responsible for dealing with her mother and that Phil would act as her support. I simply presented this format to Terry in a matter-of-fact manner. Both she and Phil agreed with the proposal. The next few sessions were devoted to devising stimulus-control strategies with Terry. Phil was encouraged to offer his input and suggestions. This made the process a team effort.

Stimulus Control and Time-Management Procedures

Terry decided that six to eight times a year were a sufficient number of visits to have with her mother. Fewer visits, she believed, would prove to be a source for conflict between the two women. Whenever possible, Terry would try to arrange for these meetings to take place in selected public settings. I suggested that she treat her mother to lunch or dinner from time to time in order to show her "gratitude." Shopping together, going to the movies, and attending church services were activities where conflicts were less likely to occur. Terry was not sure how her mother might react to these suggestions but agreed to give them a try.

More troublesome were Terry's visits to her mother's home when no other people except for her stepfather would be present. It was during such visits that she felt most anxious and vulnerable. Reducing the frequency of these visits and shortening their duration was a solution that Terry thought she could manage.

Modifying Communication and Interaction Processes: Theoretical Considerations and Pragmatic Applications

Systems theorists (Bateson, 1935; Bateson, Jackson, Haley, & Weakland, 1956; Lederer & Jackson, 1968; Watzlawick, Beavin, & Jackson, 1967) have identified three basic communication interaction patterns that are characteristic of human behavior. These are referred to as complementary, symmetrical, and parallel forms of interaction. Complementary interaction patterns are those that are characterized by verbal exchanges and behaviors that are logically opposite, such as dominance-submission, leadership-followership, and so on. In complementary patterns, the dominant person defines the nature of the relationship as one where he or she sets the rules and the submissive partner accepts this relationship definition without question. Both participants agree that the dominant partner is in charge. Symmetrical interactions are characterized by the exchange of similar or identical behaviors. Dominance is met with counterdominance, aggression is met with counteraggression, and submission is met with countersubmission. In symmetrical interactions, both partners attempt to define or redefine the relationship, set the rules, and dominate and control the other. Escalating arguments and unresolvable conflicts typify such relationships. Both complementary and symmetrical exchange patterns can become rigidly fixed, resulting in a homeostatic stalemate.

Parallel interactions are neither complementary nor symmetrical. They constitute a class of responses that are qualitatively different. Parallel responses can be used effectively to deescalate symmetrical runs and alter rigid complementary patterns. Terry was taught how to use parallel response modes to deescalate conflicts with her mother. The following is an example of such an exchange:

Mother: Terry, you didn't call me at all last week. If you cared about me, you would call me once in a while. You are very disrespectful to your mother. You are an ungrateful daughter.

Terry: Yes, Mother, I didn't call you last week, and I can understand how you would see that as disrespectful and ungrateful. How frequently would you like me to call you?

Mother: Well, at least once a week, but I should not have to tell you to call. You should want to call your mother.

Terry: I can call you once a week. I think that is a good idea.

A complementary response would be for Terry to apologize or offer excuses for not calling. A symmetrical response would be a counteraccusation that would most likely result in an argument. Terry's first response is a parallel one, which prevents a symmetrical escalation. By asking her mother how frequently she would like to receive a call from her, Terry initiates a complementary exchange. She asks a question and her mother responds, but again she attempts to engage Terry in a nonproductive (complementary or symmetrical) exchange. Terry, however, does not take the bait. She responds in a nondefensive complementary manner, which produces an outcome that is satisfactory to both mother and daughter.

The introduction of stimulus control measures, time management techniques, and deescalating response strategies made it possible for Terry to have less stressful interactions with her mother, in general. Flare-ups did occur occasionally, but they were less disconcerting, since Terry felt more in control of herself and of the process. Collusive acting out was no longer necessary, and the couple could now focus on the final PETS content area—that is, children, parenthood, and child rearing.

The couple's difficulties concerning this content area had to do with Phil's uncertainty about having his children exposed to his future mother-in-law and the volatile relationship she had with Terry. Although their relationship had improved to some extent, Phil was still skeptical and leery. When he and Terry began to date, Phil knew that Terry's relationship with her mother was strained. Conflicts between Terry and her mother increased when the couple began to live together and got worse after their engagement. Phil said that even though Terry and her mother seemed to be getting along better, his relationship with his future mother-in-law was "very bad," and he was not sure that he wanted to repair it or even if it could be repaired. Terry said that she was getting older and did not want to wait too much longer to have children. She said that if Phil could not commit to having children with her, they should reconsider their decision to marry. The couple discussed the issue of having children for several sessions, but no mutually acceptable solution concerning the couple's relationship with Terry's mother could be found. In our last session together, before the couple ended treatment, Phil said that he had been having second thoughts about having children and that he was not sure that he wanted to be a father. Terry said that Phil's statement was a "deal breaker" for her. The couple broke off their engagement several weeks later. A 6-month follow-up revealed that both Terry and Phil were involved in other relationships.

DISCUSSION

This case illustrates a number of relationship dynamics and clinical issues:

1. It has been shown in previous chapters how a presenting problem can sometimes serve as a collusive defense that couples use to avoid confronting more serious personal and relationship-threatening problems. In this case, however, the process was reversed. Terry's suggestion that the couple enroll in a less-threatening premarital education program was used to involve Phil in more difficult, critical, and substantive discussions about a topic that had been avoided for some time—the decision to have children.
2. Collusive acting out, as mentioned earlier, is a dynamic process that is not sustainable indefinitely. Eventually, some type of crisis develops, which is what often propels the couple or family into treatment. Acting out usually protects the passive spouse in that it preserves the spouse's relationship with his or her family. In this case, however, it only made matters worse for Terry. Once acting out is identified, it can be dealt with in a fairly straightforward or subtle manner. Unfortunately, sometimes irreparable damage may already have been done. When a spouse identifies "in-laws" as a problematic issue during pretreatment assessment (or on any measure), the therapist should explore this concern thoroughly. Asking the spouses to describe how they deal with their in-law problems "as a couple" can shed light on possible acting-out dynamics.
3. Scapegoating and triangulation are major components of acting out. They are critical to the maintenance of couple cohesion and personal stability, since they make it possible for the spouses to avoid dealing with unresolved issues and conflicts in their own relationship. If the therapist has been successful in

dismantling this defense, he or she should anticipate the emergence of conflicts and unresolved issues that acting out served to conceal. Phil and Terry's case is an excellent example of this process.

4. When the role of "protector" is an integral part of one's personal identity, acting out for one's spouse may become a central theme in a couple's mythology. The modification of dysfunctional conjugal themes is the subject of Chapter 8.

STUDY QUESTION

1. In each of the two case examples reviewed in this chapter, collusive acting out was brought to the couple's conscious awareness by the therapist. This interpretation then makes it difficult for the couple to deny the use of this defensive dynamic. What are some other interventional strategies that a therapist might employ to deal with such a defensive operation? Describe these strategies below and explain your reasons for choosing them.

Monitoring and Restraining: Case Example and Treatment 7

Collusive acting out is a defense that is not easily recognized at the outset of therapy. Monitoring and restraining, on the other hand, are usually identified as behaviors that are part and parcel of the presenting problem. Typically, the monitoring and restraining spouse becomes overburdened with his or her surveillance responsibilities and turns to a therapist for help. Often, the monitoring and restraining spouse behaves like a plaintiff and the monitored partner takes on the role of defendant. Maintaining therapeutic neutrality may pose a challenge, especially when some of the monitored spouse's behaviors are clearly destructive to the marriage and/or antisocial in nature. Nevertheless, the therapist must always remember that monitoring and restraining (regardless of the nature of the behaviors under consideration) still represents a collusive defense. The problematic behaviors have simply exceeded the couple's homeostatic limit. Contractual rules have been violated in some way, and a return to the previously existing equilibrium is desired. Monitoring and restraining may occur in certain specific or circumscribed areas of a couple's relationship, or it may represent a more generalized pattern.

An important assessment consideration is to determine the number of behaviors that are considered to be problematic, the frequency of their occurrence, and the context in which they are exhibited. It is also necessary to explore the person's thoughts, feelings, interpretations, and explanations about his or her problem behavior. As mentioned in Chapter 5, the monitoring and restraining spouse is genuinely upset and concerned about his or her partner's behavior, but this behavior may not be considered problematic or upsetting to the spouse who enacts it. When this is the case, prognosis for a successful therapeutic outcome is not good.

Prognosis is better for individuals who have been unaware that their behavior is a cause for concern but wish to correct it once it is brought to their attention.

When monitoring and restraining is part of the clinical picture, the therapist should try to determine whether the problem behaviors represent selected ego weaknesses, social skills deficits, superego lacunae, or a more pervasive personality pathology that includes all these factors. Making this determination will enable the therapist to help the couple set realistic therapeutic goals, given the short-term nature of the treatment. Although monitoring and restraining is an easy dynamic to diagnose, the behavior that is the focus of this process is in many cases difficult to modify, since the spouse who is the "identified patient" has been behaving problematically for most of his or her life. In some cases, internal controls and critical ego functions were never developed or were insufficiently incorporated into the spouse's personality structure. Parents, older siblings, grandparents, coaches, and others were primarily responsible for keeping problematic behaviors in check or for protecting the individual from the consequences of his or her errant behavior. Their role is then taken over by a spouse who appears to be more mature, competent, and psychologically healthy.

In the following case example, a couple I had successfully treated several years earlier (Bagarozzi, 2011) returned for treatment in order to deal with the resurfacing of their old pattern of monitoring and restraining.

CHARLES AND AMY

Summary of Previous Treatment

Amy called for an appointment for "marriage counseling" after a particularly bitter argument with her husband, Charles. When the couple entered my office, Amy began the session by saying that she was extremely angry with Charles. Charles had been unemployed for 3 months after his teaching contract with a local high school had not been renewed. Poor performance as an assistant football coach, inadequate class preparation, and conflicts with school administrators and other faculty members were cited as reasons for his termination. Amy was now solely responsible for the financial support of the couple. She was very unhappy with this arrangement, especially since Charles was not putting forth much effort to find employment. Amy, 31, and Charles, 37, had been married for 4 years. They had no children. Amy said that she was no longer willing to take responsibility for Charles, and she refused to consider having a baby until Charles could prove to her that he was a "mature adult" who was capable of being a "competent and responsible father."

Relevant Personal History

Charles

Charles was an only child. His mother had been in her late thirties when he was born; his father in his early forties. Charles' father, a former professional NFL lineman, groomed his son to play football. Charles was an outstanding athlete in high school, a star running back as well as captain of the school's track team. His coaches and teachers did whatever they could to ensure that he would maintain an acceptable GPA. His social life was closely monitored by his parents. When he was a high school senior, Charles was awarded an athletic scholarship to play college football. As had been the case in high school, his college coaches and professors made every effort to assure that he maintained academic eligibility. Tutors were provided during the school year, and employment opportunities were available during the summer. Charles' off-campus life was always under the watchful eye of assistant coaches. At home, his father assumed this responsibility.

Knee injuries prevented Charles from playing professional football. After college, he returned home to live with his parents. When his father died, Charles was set adrift. For the first time in his life, he was left without external restraints. He traveled throughout the United States, working at odd jobs to support himself, and spent a considerable amount of time in Las Vegas, where he worked as a bartender and blackjack dealer. After paying off some gambling debts, Charles moved to California. Eventually, he returned to the town where he had attended college and worked there as a bartender. It was during this time that he met Amy.

Amy

Amy was 3 years old when her father divorced her mother to marry his secretary. She had a sister four years her senior. When Amy was 9 years old, her mother remarried, but her new husband chose not to adopt Amy and her sister. Following her parents' divorce, Amy felt rejected and abandoned by her father. Her feelings of rejection were compounded by her stepfather's decision not to adopt. Her self-esteem was shattered, and she thought of herself as being unlovable, especially by men. In college, she had experimented with homosexuality but realized that her true orientation was heterosexual. Friends introduced her to Charles when she was 25 years old. After the couple had dated for approximately 6 months, she invited Charles to move in with her, and he accepted.

Relationship History

Amy had been studying for a master's degree when she and Charles met. He was tending bar at a local club. As she advanced in her career, Charles continued to work as a bartender. After about a year of living together, Amy asked Charles if he intended to marry her. He assured her that he did but did not pursue the matter. On a day when Amy was at her office and Charles was at home, Amy's mother paid him an unannounced visit. She asked him if he was planning to buy Amy an engagement ring. Charles responded that he intended to do so as soon as he had saved enough money. Amy's mother offered to "lend" Charles the funds. Charles accepted her offer and the two selected an engagement ring for Amy that very afternoon. Charles and Amy were formally engaged that evening; the couple married 6 months later.

Once married, Amy urged Charles to get a teaching certificate. She assumed the role of his tutor and was principally responsible for his successful attainment of certification. She was also instrumental in helping Charles get his first job as an assistant high school football coach. Although Amy's job responsibilities were steadily increasing, she found time to help Charles prepare for the classes he was responsible for teaching. She was also in charge of managing the couple's finances and of their social calendar. As noted earlier, when Charles's teaching contract was not renewed, Amy became entirely responsible for their financial support.

The Collusive Pact and Its Breakdown

Amy was the glue that held Charles's ego together. She curbed his impulsiveness, encouraged him when he was frustrated, structured and organized his life, and set and helped him achieve his goals. An important consideration for Amy in selecting Charles as a husband was that his dependence upon her ensured that he would not abandon or reject her. However, as time went by, taking care of Charles turned out to be more burdensome than she had anticipated. Monitoring and restraining Charles became overwhelming for her. For his part, Charles no longer found Amy's structuring of his life and their marriage to be comforting and loving. He began to experience her behavior as controlling and Amy as overbearing.

Initial Assessment Findings

LWMAT scores for Charles and Amy were 87 and 71, respectively. Amy's Disaffection score was moderate (52) while Charles's score on this measure was relatively low (31). On the other hand, Images difference scores were not very high: D = 13% for Charles and D = 14% for Amy. The couple's SIDCARB profile is presented below:

	Amy	Charles
Factor I	65	60
Factor II	30	60
Factor III	43	45

A moderate power discrepancy existed. Amy perceived fewer barriers to divorce than did Charles. Trust, as measured by the Relationship Trust Scale, showed that Amy had some major misgivings about Charles in terms of his dependability. She responded "strongly disagree" to these two items: "I can rely upon my partner to keep the promises he/she makes to me" and "Even though my partner makes excuses that sound unlikely, I am confident that he/she is telling the truth." When asked about her responses, Amy revealed that Charles had had a gambling problem and that she had to remain vigilant. This was Amy's major reason for taking responsibility for the couple's financial affairs. Scores for both Amy and Charles on "total intimacy needs strength" were quite low—279 for Amy and 368 for Charles. Nevertheless Amy was dissatisfied with both "receptivity and reciprocity" for Charles in the areas of emotional, psychological, and sexual intimacy, while Charles's only concern on this measure was with social and recreational intimacy.

When I asked Charles about his thoughts and feelings concerning Amy's complaints, he said that some of them were justified but many were "blown out of proportion" and that Amy tended to be "a little anal." However, he did acknowledge some need for change.

INTERVENTION

At the outset of treatment, I assured Amy and Charles that the anger they were experiencing was understandable given their current life circumstances. I added that, in many cases, the spouses' well-intentioned but unilateral attempts to solve their problems could serve only to compound them. Offering these observations helped to ensure that neither spouse would feel blamed or accused, and established therapeutic neutrality.

Defusing the couple's anger was the next step. To do this, I explained that prolonged anger between spouses would eventually have a corrosive effect upon the marriage. I suggested that the couple might be better served by "transforming" this anger into "determination" and using this to learn some basic communication and conflict negotiation skills that might serve to deal with the couple's problems. The acceptance of this reframing helped to redirect the couple's negative affect. It also paved the way for the dismantling of the collusive pact that had served to maintain their enmeshment. A strategy was then devised to help Amy and Charles function more autonomously, without threatening the security of their marriage. To underscore the solidity of the couple's relationship, I referred to their SIDCARB profile, noting that there were few barriers to relationship termination, that both spouses perceived their marriage to be voluntary, and that they were both committed to remaining together and improving their relationship. By focusing on the positive and voluntary nature of the marriage and stressing the couple's commitment to change, the stability and security of the relationship was affirmed and given support by objective and empirical findings. This set the stage for more independent and less enmeshed personal functioning for both Amy and Charles.

As mentioned previously, during the early stages of a marriage, the spouse who is the focus of monitoring and restraining may experience this oversight as an indication of love, caring, concern, and so on. Eventually, such supervision becomes oppressive and is seen as controlling, and both partners become frustrated and angry. It is precisely at this time that a couple will be open to suggestions that they begin to function more autonomously, especially if they believe that their marriage is strong enough to withstand more personal freedom and independence. Reframing this need for autonomy as a normal stage in a couple's development gives the therapist some leverage in dealing with the monitoring and restraining dynamic.

Charles and Amy acknowledged and agreed that the way their lives had been structured was no longer functional or desirable and that a change was necessary. They both agreed with the interpretation that Amy's attempts to help Charles had become burdensome for her and were experienced as intrusive and controlling by him. The therapeutic issue then became one of how to change the established pattern in a way that would also take into account each spouse's unique personal issues (that is, Amy's fear of abandonment and feelings of being defective and unworthy of a man's love, and Charles's need for external structure and ego strengthening—as regards goal-setting, following through on task completion, impulse control, and frustration tolerance). This process was begun by helping the couple develop a cooperative strategy that would allow Charles to explore employment opportunities on his own but would also permit Amy to participate in this process in a way that was acceptable to her and that Charles would not experience as intrusive or controlling.

To further facilitate the spouses' independent functioning, I asked Charles to consider a referral to a colleague whose specialty was social skills training so that Charles could enhance his job interviewing skills. The rationale offered for this suggestion was that since Charles's problematic behavior at his last job was partially responsible for his termination, social skills training might prove to be of some value to him. At first, Charles balked at this suggestion, but after two unsuccessful job interviews he reconsidered and followed through with the referral. Charles's involvement in social skills training was liberating for Amy, and she began to feel less responsible for monitoring and correcting her husband. Now that these procedures were in place, I turned my attention to Amy.

Amy's feelings of low self-esteem came predominantly from a sense of worthlessness rather than a lack of competence. She was very successful in her chosen career and had received a number of recognition awards from her colleagues. Her feelings of low self-worth were rooted in her ambivalent relationship with her father. To begin, Amy completed the Multidimensional Self-Esteem Inventory: MSEI (O'Brien & Epstein, 1988). Two subscales were particularly important for her: lovability and likeability. She attributed her low scores on these two dimensions as having been influenced by her relationship with her father, who she believed did not value her.

Amy's contact with her father over the years had been brief and superficial, even though they lived within an hour's driving distance from each other. I suggested to Amy that possibly her long-held belief that her father did not value her might not be altogether accurate—that it might be an "irrational belief" in need of testing. I asked her if she would consider having some sessions with her father in order to test her assumptions. She agreed to this, with full encouragement from Charles, who voiced positive feelings about his father-in-law.

The sessions between Amy and her father were highly emotional but constructive. He explained that the limited involvement he had had with her as a child was the result of the contentious relationship he had with Amy's mother rather than any negative feelings he had toward his daughter. To the contrary, he added that he tried to protect her and had done all he could to avoid letting Amy become entangled in her parents' disagreements over child support and visitation. He said that he loved and respected Amy and admired her achievements. She was both shocked and pleased when her father offered her a position with his company.

Amy's acceptance of this offer opened a new chapter in her life. Her father's support, encouragement, praise, and genuine affection had a profound effect upon her feelings of self-worth. As for Charles, owing to the progress he made and the goals he achieved through his social skills training classes, Charles had developed enough self-confidence to apply for another coaching/teaching position in a neighboring school district. He was successful in his application and received a 1-year probationary contract. Renewal was contingent upon his performance and evaluations from superiors.

At this juncture, Amy and Charles had made sufficient progress to bring therapy to an end. The only area in which monitoring and restraining still existed was Amy's concern about Charles's possible return to excessive gambling. I pointed out that they had made great strides in learning to function autonomously. I added, however, that their "old pattern" (i.e., monitoring and restraining) still lingered with regard to Charles's gambling. Both Charles and Amy agreed that if Charles's gambling were to become a problem again, they would seek professional help.

Charles and Amy: A Year Later

When Amy contacted me for an appointment 13 months after she and Charles had concluded treatment, I expected to hear that Charles's gambling had again become a problem. I was wrong. The presenting problem this time was Amy's concern about Charles's relationship with a female colleague. After initial greetings and a brief review of the past year's activities, I asked Amy and Charles to discuss the problem from their own unique perspectives.

Amy: Dr. Bagarozzi, I think Charles has developed too close a relationship with one of his coworkers, Tricia. I think their relationship is inappropriate and unhealthy.

Therapist: What about their relationship do you believe is inappropriate and unhealthy?

Amy: They spend too much time together at work and after the school day is over. They meet at the health club, and they have had dinner together when I've been out of town. Charles also talks to her about our marriage, even sometimes about our sex life.

Therapist: Charles, how do you see this situation?

Charles: She talks like I'm screwing Tricia. I'm not. She is just a good friend. Amy has a lot of guy friends, and I'm not jealous.

Amy: But I don't spend a lot of time with my male friends. I don't meet them for dinner, and I certainly don't talk about our sex life with them.

Therapist: Charles, can you tell me a little about your friendship with Tricia?

Charles: She teaches English, and she has her master's degree in special ed. She has won the outstanding teacher award twice, and she used to run track when she was in high school.

Therapist: She sounds like a pretty accomplished woman. I see you have some things in common. You both ran track, if I remember correctly?

Charles: Yes, we did.

Therapist: What is it about Tricia that makes her such a good friend?

Amy: She's got big boobs and a tight butt!

Charles: You see, Dr. B., this is what I mean. She thinks I have the hots for Tricia. Sure, she is good-looking, but that's not why I'm friends with her.

Therapist: What other qualities, aside from her good looks, does Tricia have that make her a good friend?

Charles: In my last job, I had problems with class management and class preparation. Tricia has been a really big help to me in these two areas. When I have a problem with students, I can talk to her. She's always got some good suggestions. She has also been helpful with my class preparation, so to show my appreciation, I bought her dinner one time.

Amy: That all sounds good, Charles, but it doesn't explain why you talk to her about our sex life. I'll bet she can give you some good ideas there, too! Maybe even teach you a few things!

Charles: Doc, this is hopeless. I swear, I am not having sex with Tricia.

Amy: That's what Bill Clinton said!

Charles: Doc, help me out here. I know you don't take sides, but I can't prove a negative. Do you have any suggestions?

Therapist: I try my best not to take sides, but there is a difference between taking sides and pointing out what theory and research have shown to be functional and dysfunctional in a marriage. You remember when we first started to work together. I taught you how to communicate successfully. The guidelines I gave to you were based upon theory and years of clinical research. Now, I can share with you what we know about functional and dysfunctional marital structures and processes. You may wish to make some changes in your marriage based upon what I have to offer.

Charles: OK.

Amy: (Nods head.)

Therapist: You may recall when we first worked together, learning to separate a little and function more independently was seen as a developmental stage that posed a problem for you. You seem to have mastered that task fairly well. The task that faces you now has to do with defining systems boundaries.

Charles: What do you mean? I don't understand.

Amy: Neither do I.

Therapist: I'll try to explain. Do you remember when we worked with the Intimacy Needs Questionnaire? (Hands Amy and Charles their Intimacy Needs Questionnaires.)

Charles: Yes

Amy: Yes.

Therapist: The strength of a need in each component area determines how comfortable you are with intimacy or interpersonal closeness in that particular area. We erect boundaries for each component area to protect the self from being intruded upon. These are referred to as personal or ego boundaries. Do you understand me so far?

Amy: Yes.

Charles: Yes.

Therapist: The person then decides what information about the self is appropriate to disclose; that is, what information is permitted to pass through these personal boundaries. Well, the same is true for marriages. All couples must come to some agreement about their own boundaries—what they consider to be intrusive and what information about their relationship is appropriate to share with outsiders. Boundary erection and maintenance is a critical task for couples. It seems to me that you and Charles may not be very clear about your systems boundaries.

Amy: Well, I'm clear about one thing. No sex with anyone else.

Charles: I agree.

Amy: I'm not so sure.

Charles: I have never done that in all the time we've been together. You know that's true. This is a small town and a small high school. If we were screwing around, the word would be out in a minute. You know that, and I think you are blowing things out of proportion because she is pretty and for no other reason. You are not jealous of my relationship with Amanda, because she is not very attractive. You are just insecure because of what your father did to your mother. That's what I think.

Amy: Maybe you're right, but I still want you to limit your contact with Tricia.

Charles: What do you want me to do?

Amy: Cut out the extracurricular activity.

Charles: Do you want me to tell her that you don't want me to be friends with her?

Amy: I don't care what you tell her. Just stop it!

Charles: If I tell her you are jealous, she'll think you are paranoid.

Amy: I don't care what she thinks of me. I know what I think about her. Just quit it!

Charles: OK. I'll handle it.

Therapist: Charles, before you do or say anything to Tricia, I think it would be helpful if you and Amy could reach some type of an agreement about relationships with members of the opposite sex—what is appropriate and what is not. I also think it is very important for you to decide what information about your relationship you will share with others. Once you have done this, you can restructure your relationship with Tricia in a way that will be acceptable to both of you.

Charles: OK.

Amy: OK.

DISCUSSION

The presenting problem for Charles and Amy when they came in for the second time was Amy's jealousy. Although different in content, the dynamic between the spouses was still monitoring and restraining. Whether Charles had been having an affair with Tricia or whether they were, as Charles had sworn, "good friends," could never be determined. What was evident, however, was that Tricia had adopted Amy's monitoring and restraining role in the workplace. She also provided structure and guidance in that setting. Using others to compensate for ego weakness and/or deficits can be considered a stimulus control measure, a quasi-self-monitoring and restraining technique, that is successful only as long as others are present. Without the aid of these external agents, problem behaviors are likely to reemerge, since internal controls have not been developed. For example, when either Amy or Tricia was present, Charles's ability to tolerate frustration was increased, impulse control was kept in check, and his ability to postpone gratification was improved. He relied upon both women for help with his judgment and planning and to speculate about the future consequences of his actions. However, when they were not present to serve as monitors and restrainers, these deficits would come to the fore.

The reality of such collusive defensive arrangements is that without more concentrated and extended therapy designed to ameliorate selected ego deficits and weaknesses, monitoring and restraining will continue to play a significant role in the relationship. How long the monitoring and restraining spouse will accept the arrangement depends upon the needs of that spouse. As Amy's self-confidence and self-esteem improved and she and Charles began to function more independently, Amy felt less responsible for Charles's behavior. One can speculate that Charles's involvement with Tricia was one way of forcing Amy to become more intimately involved with him, thus reestablishing their previous equilibrium. Amy's response to Charles's relationship with Tricia was understandable, given her family history. My discussion with the couple about systems boundaries was designed to help place their difficulties within the context of a normal developmental challenge, but it did not deal with the monitoring and restraining dynamic and Charles's ego weaknesses that this process was meant to remedy. These issues were addressed in the final session.

Therapist: Well, folks, It seems that you have been able to reach an agreement about your relationship boundaries, especially as these relate to Tricia.

Amy: Pretty much.

Charles: It's a done deal.

Therapist: Charles, when you say it is a done deal, what do you mean?

Charles: We agree on what my relationship will be with Tricia. It is limited to work. No extracurricular stuff.

Amy: We'll see. Time will tell.

Therapist: Charles, it seems that you have been relying upon other people to help you structure some important aspects of your life. Amy, you have taken on much of this responsibility in the past, and this has created problems for both of you.

Now, I think some of this responsibility has been transferred to Tricia, at least as far as your job is concerned, and this has become a problem in your marriage. Charles, I am concerned that if you don't learn how to take on these responsibilities for yourself, that you will continue to have problems personally and as a couple.

Amy: I agree.

Charles: What do you suggest, Doc?

Therapist: I suggest that you return to Dr. Holland to continue your work on social skills development. I know that he has helped you in the past and that you liked working with him.

Amy: I think this is a good idea.

Charles: Maybe, but I'm not ready to do it just now. Maybe at some time in the future.

DISCUSSION

Short-term problem-focused marital therapy is not the optimal context for helping individuals strengthen and acquire critical ego functions. An individually tailored cognitive behavioral self-control approach that targets specific ego functions is more appropriate. The length of treatment will vary depending upon the number of ego functions to be strengthened and/or acquired. Individual or group settings should be used whenever possible so as to reduce the other spouse's continued participation in the monitoring and restraining process. It is also important to understand the benefit the monitoring and restraining spouse derived from his or her involvement, so that a more functional and rewarding alternative marital role can be developed.

It is also important to determine whether one is dealing with isolated ego deficits and superego lacunae or whether one is confronted with a definite constellation of ego problems and superego failings symptomatic of a severe personality disorder, which could require long-term intensive therapy or inpatient treatment (Piper & Joyce, 2001).

It is also necessary to take into account a person's ethnic and cultural background in evaluating ego and superego functioning. For example, an aggressive response to frustration may be interpreted as poor impulse control, poor judgment, an inability to differentiate between aggression and assertion, an inability to bind anxiety and use it constructively, and so forth. However, this response to frustration may be considered perfectly normal, understandable, and acceptable in some ethnic groups and subcultures. In such cases, these behaviors are ego-syntonic for the individual and do not represent a problem or deficit in his or her subculture. The person's failure to recognize that these behaviors are problematic does not stem from a lack of empathy or faulty role-taking ability but simply represents how one has learned to respond in certain situations. It may be an integral part of one's role as a man/woman, husband/wife, or father/mother.

Similarly, monitoring and restraining one's spouse may also represent a subcultural norm, and neither spouse may see it as a cause for concern. Monitoring and restraining often occurs in response to an extramarital affair. This is to be expected in a marriage for a time until trust is regained (Bagarozzi, 2008). This phenomenon should be differentiated from the collusive monitoring and restraining used to protect the partners' respective selves and maintain dyadic homeostasis. Monitoring and restraining is common in marriages where there is alcoholism and substance abuse. This dynamic can become so ingrained in a couple's mode of functioning that it continues even after the addicted spouse is clean and sober. Similarly, monitoring and restraining can become a way of responding to a spouse's or partner's compulsive behavior (e.g., pornography, gambling, overeating). In these cases, referral to a professional who specializes in the treatment of such conditions is warranted. In all cases where monitoring and restraining has come to define a couple's relationship, the therapist must try to understand how both spouses benefit from the collusion and how monitoring and restraining preserves the marriage. Having such understanding will make it possible for the therapist to help the couple set realistic and achievable treatment goals. Individual and group treatments can be valuable adjuncts to marital therapy when monitoring and restraining is present.

STUDY QUESTION

1. The interventions used with Amy and Charles were educational, behavioral, and intergenerational. Since insightful interpretations could do little to strengthen the ego deficits that Charles presented, a social skills–training approach focusing on selected ego weaknesses was included as an adjunct to marital therapy. However, Charles's reluctance to return for additional work in this area did not bode well for the couple. Although Amy was still motivated to improve her relationship with Charles, she was becoming more frustrated with him as her self-esteem increased. Given the fact that both spouses perceived few barriers to relationship termination, divorce was a distinct possibility if their situation did not improve. Keeping these factors in mind, what course of action would you pursue with Charles and Amy at this juncture?

Complementary Defensive Systems: Couple Mythologies 8

Up to this point, the focus of this text has been the simple collusive pacts that spouses devise to protect each other and maintain dyadic stability. In this chapter, a more complex and elaborate type of defensive arrangement is reviewed—one that entails the complementary meshing of defensive themes from the personal life histories of each partner. This collusive system has been referred to earlier as a couple's mythology (Bagarozzi & Anderson, 1989).

Personal myths exist in all of us and serve the function of explaining and guiding our behavior in a manner similar to the role played by cultural and religious myths. The self is the architect of one's personal mythology—giving meaning to past experiences, maintaining continuity and integrity, defining the present, and providing guidance and direction for the future. Personal myths are complexes of symbolic and affectively laden roles, scripts, and themes that are made up of three basic components: the self, the selves of others, and the self in relation to other selves. One's interpersonal style of relating to others evolves as one attempts to master and resolve the various developmental tasks and interpersonal conflicts that inevitably arise during each stage of the life cycle. The more difficulty one has in overcoming a particular developmental challenge, the more the task will persist as a motive for resolution throughout one's life. Essentially it becomes a recurrent theme in one's personal mythology. Attempts to rework and overcome these conflicts manifest themselves through a variety of transferential dynamics. Frequently, people select lovers, partners, spouses, and so on who they believe will allow them to play out these unresolved conflictual issues by enacting complementary roles, scripts, and themes. This is often a reciprocal process. The unconscious dovetailing of complementary roles, scripts, and themes is central to a couple's mythological system. A couple's mythology may consist of one or two interrelated themes. In some instances, a half dozen or more themes may be involved.

It would be incorrect and misleading to think of all themes in a couple's mythology as being problematic. For example, a man who marries a nurturant woman to make up for his parents' neglect may be a very suitable partner for a woman whose parents and siblings valued her family role as a kind and considerate child. On the other hand, some couple themes may be dysfunctional in the sense that their enactment damages the selves of the participants and curtails the growth and development of the couple system. These are the subject of this chapter. Like personal defensive operations, dysfunctional couple themes are used to protect the self and preserve dyadic equilibrium.

JOHN AND SARA

John called for an appointment for "marriage counseling." He said that he and his wife had been "quarreling" and "not communicating well lately." They needed some help "listening to each other." John, 29, and Sara, 27, had been married for 4 years and had no children. Sara was a paralegal and John was an I.T. specialist. John had called on a Tuesday, and I gave him an appointment for the following Wednesday is the next day. A day before their scheduled visit, John called to postpone their session. Sara had come down with the flu, and he did not know when she would be well enough to meet with me. About 10 days later, John called again and another appointment was arranged. This appointment also had to be rescheduled when Sara had to undergo a minor surgical procedure. I finally met with the couple 4 weeks after John's initial telephone contact.

When John and Sara arrived at my office, they both seemed tired. John said that neither of them had slept well the night before. Both were anxious about "going into counseling." I said: "Well, you have taken the first step and that is usually the hardest part." This seemed to put them at ease.

Sara was a frail, petite woman who spoke in a very soft voice. John was a short, slender man with pale skin and dark eyes. Sara wore a long black skirt and a white blouse that was buttoned to her throat. Even though it was a warm spring day, she wore a dark-gray knitted vest. John wore loose-fitting green slacks, brown shoes, a blue shirt, and a yellow tie.

I began the session by asking the couple if they could "tell me a little about the problem." Sara was the first to speak. She said that she and John had not been getting along lately, and that he had become more distant over the past few months. John then explained that he had recently taken a new job; he was working longer hours and could not spend as much time with Sara as both of them would have preferred. He added that with his new job and increased responsibilities, he did not think that the situation would change very much in the near future. John said, "We used to spend a lot of time together. Now, that's changed." Sara said, "I know it's crazy, but it's like he has chosen his job over me. That's sick, isn't it?" I said, "My job is not to label you. My job is to help you understand and to help you change those things that are within your power to change." I tried to normalize the couple's problem by adding that their situation was not an uncommon one and was part of a couple's "developmental process." Sara said, "So we are not hopeless?" I smiled and said, "No, I don't think so."

Relevant Personal History

John

John had grown up in the Midwest. Both his parents were schoolteachers. He had one sibling, a sister, who was 2 years his senior. John described his childhood as "normal" and his family as supportive and loving. His parents rarely quarreled, and growing up was "easy." His hometown was small; "everyone knew everyone else." Life was simple and good until, when John was 15, a riding accident left his sister partially paralyzed. From that point on, everything changed, and John became one of his sister's caretakers. A sadness hung over the family. John put off going to college so that he could remain at home a little longer to help care for his sister. Reluctantly, John left for college when he was 19. His parents and sister were supportive of his leaving, but John was ambivalent. At times he thought of himself as a person who had deserted his family. This characterization was not consistent with his self-image, and his self-esteem suffered. What made matters worse was the fact that there were no employment opportunities available for John in his hometown once he completed his education. To have a successful career, John would have to live in a large city. John was conflicted. Was he a responsible and loyal family member who would help care for his sister, or was he a selfish deserter? These questions remained as central themes in his personal mythology and caused him to become depressed from time to time.

Sara

Sara was the youngest of three daughters. Her father was a surgeon and her mother had been a nurse. After her parents married, Sara's mother worked in her father's medical office until their first child was born. She then became a "stay-at-home mom." Sara referred to her parents as "orthodox Catholics" who used the "rhythm" (i.e., natural family planning) method of birth control. Sara was an "accident." She said that her parents were not very sexual people. Sex was for procreation. Sexual activity for pleasure was considered concupiscence. Her home was run like a hospital or medical practice. Her mother's role was to make sure that the children did not disturb or upset their father. He was the hub of the family and everything revolved around him. He was a distant man without much warmth. Roles were rigidly fixed in Sara's family. Mary, the eldest daughter, was the studious bookworm who later became a pediatrician. Shannon, the middle child, was the athlete. She became a high school teacher and a girls' basketball coach. Sara was the "sick child." Shannon called her "sickly Sara." Both parents were concerned about Sara's health. She had asthma, food and pet allergies, and was accident-prone. Shannon said that Sara used her illnesses to compete with her sisters for their father's attention. To Sara, being taken care of meant being nurtured and loved. This became a central theme in her personal mythology. Whether she became ill or accidentally injured herself made no difference. What was important to her was the connection it forged with others, particularly her father. However, the unconscious symbolic meaning of her accident-proneness was much less obvious. It served as a subtle reminder to Sara and her parents that she had been "an accident." The underlying thematic question about her worthiness was more profound.

Identifying Salient Themes in the Couple's Mythology

In John and Sara's case, two dovetailing personal themes—caretaking and illness and their accompanying roles and scripts—were identified as a conjugal theme, but the defensive aspects of this complementary meshing was not immediately addressed. Theme identification is the first step in the therapeutic process. Whenever possible, assessment findings should be used to support theme identification. This is done by first reviewing all assessment instruments and selecting those items that are germane to the themes under consideration. Since Images (Anderson, Bagarozzi, & Giddings, 1986) deals with specific marital role expectations and discrepancies, two items directly related to the conjugal theme of caretaking and illness were selected for discussion. For Sara, item 19, "My spouse is very much like my father" was chosen. For John, item 20, "My spouse is very much like my sister" was used. Initially, only the positive aspects of a conjugal theme are interpreted and positively reframed. For example, I suggested that perhaps the caretaking and illness dynamic might be a unique way that the couple had devised to reconnect whenever John became too distant, like Sara's father. Sara's illnesses, at such times, became a type of barometer signaling that the couple had drifted too far apart. I referred to these illnesses as "love sicknesses." I also suggested that perhaps John's periodic depression might cause him to become distant, but he could not be depressed for too long if Sara became ill. He would have to attend to Sara. Her illness, therefore, would pull him out of his depression by activating his caretaking role, the role he had played vis-à-vis his sister. Caretaking and illness then took on a very different meaning for the couple.

Most couples will be receptive to exploring the less positive and defensive dimensions of conjugal themes if they are characterized as the couple's unsuccessful attempts to deal with universal marital/family developmental challenges—in this case, negotiating mutually acceptable levels of closeness and distance.

Dysfunctional marital themes are simply more complex defensive systems that have evolved over time to protect and validate the self and preserve the couple's homeostatic balance. Conjugal themes are not static entities and can be modified by editing one or more of their constituent components. The focus of intervention can be one spouse's personal theme, the personal themes of both spouses, or the conjugal theme itself. A change in any component will necessitate a change in all other components. Editing can be done directly or indirectly. Some of the most common forms of direct intervention are interpretation, cognitive restructuring, role creation, and role enactment. Positive reframing, the use of analogies, telling metaphorical stories, and giving ritual prescriptions constitute less-direct approaches.

Once a characteristic thematic interaction sequence has been identified and positively reframed, it is labeled a "communication channel" that has outlived its usefulness. For example, caretaking and illness were interpreted as once being used to achieve closeness and intimacy and to express "love and affection" (an item appearing on SIDCARB), but this channel was described as "no longer functional." A new channel had to be opened. I said that learning more direct ways of communicating and meeting these needs would help the couple acquire new and more satisfying channels for expressing love and receiving affection.

John and Sara were taught how to identify their characteristic caretaking and illness interaction pattern and how to alter it once they had recognized that the cycle had begun. A couple's interaction around a conjugal theme is viewed systemically; it is redundant and circular and can be arrested at any point in the cycle. For example, John's withdrawal and distancing (for whatever reason), Sara's becoming ill or having an accident, John's caretaking and concern, and so on are all part of the same circular process. The new interaction pattern that the couple create together is then labeled and becomes a more functional conjugal theme. For John and Sara, the more satisfying interaction pattern consisted of (1) becoming aware of their feelings, needs, and desires; (2) communicating these to each other; and (3) responding to the partner's expressed feelings, needs, desires, and requests. This thematic pattern was labeled "awareness-communicate-respond."

In order to help John and Sara integrate their new thematic communication interaction pattern into their everyday lives, in-session practice and coaching exercises, combined with homework assignments, were used to address their anxieties about entering therapy. Taking into consideration Sara's concerns about the prospects for their marriage, I characterized the work to be done as a learning experience, as opposed to being a therapeutic one. To present the clinical experience in an encouraging light, I referred to the assessment findings. I said to Sara and John that even though their scores on the Dyadic Adjustment Scale were in the distressed range, their Disaffection scores were very low, indicating strong positive emotional attachments, and that their Trust Scale scores were very high. I pointed out that their SIDCARB profile showed their relationship to be a mildly distressed yet voluntary marriage, with only three areas of moderate conflict—communication, in-laws, and expressions of love and affection—and that the last of these concerns was echoed in their Intimacy Needs Questionnaire findings. I pointed out that their ability to communicate their needs and respond to each other's requests for more closeness, distance, affection, and so on had been improving steadily with the introduction of the more satisfying awareness-communicate-respond thematic pattern. I then expressed my belief that the couple might be ready to tackle the mutually agreed upon SIDCARB area of concern, in-laws. They agreed.

Editing Personal Themes and Modifying the Self Structure

After a conjugal theme has been successfully edited and becomes part of the couple's new way of interacting, those vulnerable aspects of the self that the old thematic pattern once protected must be addressed. Dramatic changes in the self structure are not the goal of short-term, brief forms of marital therapy and should not be expected, but modest changes in the self structure can be brought about by editing central themes in an individual's personal mythology.

When a personal theme is identified, the therapist must determine what aspect or aspects of the self the theme is designed to protect. Does the theme deal with one's worthiness? Does the theme deal with one's competence? Does the theme deal with both worthiness and competence? These are the central questions to be answered.

As discussed in Chapter 2, self-esteem comprises two major components: worthiness and competence. The more one's perceived self approximates his or her ideal self, the higher the person's self-esteem will be. Sometimes a theme in one's personal mythology develops as a way of defending against the negative emotions engendered by significant perceived discrepancies between the self and the ideal self. The Multidimensional Self-Esteem Inventory, or MSEI (O'Brien & Epstein, 1988), can be a very useful tool to help individuals identify such discrepancies. The MSEI is a theoretically derived and empirically validated self-report measure consisting of three fairly independent factors:

> Factor I: Overall self-esteem and effectance, which corresponds with competence
> Factor II: Social self-esteem, which corresponds with worthiness
> Factor III: Defensive self-esteem, which represents a self-protective, overly inflated view of the self

Subcomponents for Factor I are competence (10 items), self-control (10 items), and identity integration (10 items). Subcomponents for Factor II are lovability (10 items) and likeability (10 items). The following subcomponents had items that cross-loaded on Factors I and II: global self-esteem (10 items), personal power (10 items), body appearance (10 items), and body functioning (10 items). Moral self-approval (10 items) is considered to be a "private self-evaluation" by the authors and loads on the third factor, defensiveness (26 items). Whether the person's responses to the items that constitute moral self-approval represent a true self-appraisal or whether they portray defensive self-posturing is difficult to know. However, a thorough personal history that incorporates the 16 questions outlined in Chapter 2 can be helpful in making this determination.

MSEI profile scores are plotted on a scoring grid. T scores are used, which have a mean of 50 and a standard deviation of 10. Scores that fall within one standard deviation above or below the mean are considered to be in the normal range. T scores of two standard deviations above the mean represent moderately high levels of self-esteem, whereas scores two standard deviations below the mean are indicative of moderately low levels of self-esteem.

John's guilt over his self-described "desertion" of his family was reflected in moderately low levels of self-esteem scores for lovability, likeability, and moral self-approval. For Sara, global self-esteem, lovability, personal power, and body functioning were in the moderately low range.

INTERVENTIONS

John's sense of worth was rooted in his self-definition as a loving, caring, responsible person and loyal family member. This self-definition found its expression through his role as caretaker and by becoming responsible for the well-being and safety of others. Perceived and ideal-self definitions were closely aligned until John left home. The longer he was away from his family, the more he experienced a discrepancy between these two structural components of himself. The guilt he felt as a result of his "desertion" was assuaged to some degree when he resumed his caretaking role with Sara, but this did not address the underlying issue of divided loyalties. John's self-esteem problem only became worse when the couple's relationship began to improve after the introduction of the more functional thematic interaction pattern of awareness-communicate-respond.

Sara's more assertive requests for intimate time with John and the reduced frequency of her illnesses and accidents allowed the couple to spend more pleasurable time together. Devoting his time to a sickly wife justified John's "neglect" of his family of origin; but as the couple's relationship theme of caretaking and illness became less pronounced, John's guilt increased.

Both worthiness and competence were issues for Sara. The relationship between these two components of self-esteem was a complex one. Sara had always believed that in order for her to receive love and affection from her parents, she had to be sickly and incompetent—that is, accident-prone. Her role as "sickly Sara" was firmly fixed in the family dynamic. Although this self-definition was undergoing some modification in her relationship with John, she did not know how her parents and sisters would react to such a change, since Sara's health concerns were a frequent topic of conversation whenever she and John visited her family.

When one's parents, siblings, and other significant family members are available, an intergenerational approach can be a very effective means for bringing about some modifications in the structural components of the self. For this reason, I asked the couple to focus on the SIDCARB item "in-laws." I said that based upon the couple's initial discussion of SIDCARB items, I knew that visits with both sets of parents were a source of considerable stress. I suggested that perhaps I could help them find a way to make these visits less stressful. An excerpt from the couple's discussion of this issue is provided below.

Therapist: The holidays are coming up soon, and I know that you will be visiting your parents and spending some time with them. What do you see as the most troubling aspects of these visits?

Sara: I'll start. John, I know this sounds selfish, but when we visit your parents, I feel neglected. You spend a lot of time with Katie, and I feel left out.

John: I know I do. I don't mean to neglect you, but I don't get to see her very much. We talk on the phone, and we e-mail, but that's not the same thing.

Sara: Well, it's not only that. It's how you get after we leave. You get depressed a lot of the time when we leave.

John: Sometimes it is depressing. Katie doesn't have much of a life. She's got her work and some friends, but no husband, no children. Facebook is a poor substitute for a life.

Therapist: In my work, I don't get to see such devotion to one's family very often. I think I know how hard it was for you to leave your family, especially Katie. You've referred to your leaving as desertion. That's a pretty harsh label. I think there might be some sort of disconnect between how you saw yourself then, when you lived with your family, and how you see yourself now. Perhaps you are trying to live up to some unrealistic expectation or standard.

John: I don't know. Maybe.

Therapist: Leaving home is a developmental milestone that can be bittersweet for many people. There is the hope and promise for the future and the sadness of leaving loved ones. Sometimes we may feel disloyal, and this will affect our relationship with our partners. It can prevent us from being truly intimate in many areas of marriage.

John: Dr. B., I don't think Sara really appreciates how I feel. Nobody in her family is close. Don't get me wrong, they are nice people, but unemotional and detached.

Therapist: John, if I remember correctly, Katie and your parents encouraged you to attend college, and then they supported your decision to move here. Wasn't that the case?

John: Yes, they did.

Therapist: Do you think their encouragement was sincere?

John: Yes, I know it was.

Therapist: Yet you still feel guilty for not returning to your hometown where you could be close to your family.

John: Correct.

Therapist: I don't doubt that what you say about your parents and your sister is true, so I don't understand the reasons for your guilt. Can you help me out a little?

Sara: Dr. B., John feels responsible for Katie's accident.

John: She's right, Dr. B., I do blame myself to some degree.

Therapist: John, can you tell me what happened on the day of Katie's accident?

John: The day of the accident, she asked me if I would like to go riding with her. It was a Saturday, and I said I'd rather sleep in than ride horses. Two hours later, we got the call from the hospital. Katie was in intensive care, in critical condition. The horse had broken its leg and had to be put down. I've often thought that if I had been with her, she might not have taken the risks she did that day. When we rode together, she taught me to ride; she was always concerned about my safety and never did anything risky. I know she would have been more cautious if I had been with her.

Therapist: And you blame yourself.

John: I know that's not logical.

Therapist: No, but it is psychological and makes sense from that perspective.

John: Sometimes I dream that Katie and I are adults, like we are now, and we are riding together again, and she is fine. Sometimes I dream of the accident and I'm not there to help her.

Therapist: John, have you talked with Katie or your parents about your feelings of guilt about the accident?

John: Not directly. I've told Katie I was sorry I had not been there to help her, but that's about it.

Therapist: You might consider talking to them about these feelings on your next visit.

John: I need to think about that for awhile.

DISCUSSION

After discussing this prospect with Sara, John decided that he would be willing to talk with his sister and parents about his feelings concerning Katie's accident. John thought it would be easier for him to talk with Katie and his parents separately, without Sara being present for these discussions. Sara was agreeable and said she would be available to support him in any way he thought necessary.

Two interrelated issues having to do with John's sense of worthiness had to be addressed: perceived self/ideal self discrepancies and the guilt that these discrepancies produced. The next two sessions were devoted to helping the couple prepare for the upcoming visit to John's parents. When John thought the time was right, he planned to ask Katie how she felt about his not accompanying her on the day of her accident and how she felt about his not being there to help her. He also had decided to ask her how she felt about his not returning home after he graduated from college and to ask his sister for her forgiveness. The focus of John's talks with his parents would be different. He wanted to know whether they were disappointed in him and whether they perceived him to be a disloyal deserter.

How parents label and treat a child affects how that child begins to perceive himself or herself. Eventually these labels become part of the child's self-definition. Models held up for the child's emulation become part of the child's ideal self. In the best of all possible worlds, these labels are positive, consistent with the child's experience of himself or herself, and the ideal self is realistic and attainable. In reality, however, such trifold congruence is rare. A number of difficulties can arise that cause disequilibrium in the self structure. For example, as the child grows older, he or she may become aware that the introjected self-definition is not congruent with how he or she actually feels and experiences himself or herself to be. Essentially, there is a discrepancy between what he or she knows to be the true self and the distorted self-definition that he or she had uncritically accepted. Sometimes, there may be significant differences between the parents' and the child's interpretation of the same label. For example, in John's case, his definition of "a responsible son" (i.e., his ideal self) was quite different from his parents' use of this term. By discussing his concerns with his parents, these discrepancies could be addressed.

John and Sara visited his parents for the Thanksgiving holiday and were not seen in therapy for 2 weeks. When they returned, John reported that their stay with his family had gone well. He said that his parents were surprised when he told them that he had felt like a "disloyal son" who had "deserted" them. They reassured him that this was not the case and that their expectations for him had always been that he would move away from home, marry, and have a family of his own. They added that his primary responsibilities were to Sara and to his children once they were born. His responsibilities to his parents and sister were for him to keep in touch, to visit them from time to time, and open his home to them when they came to visit.

John's talks with Katie had been much more emotional. She said that she certainly did not hold him in any way responsible for her accident. What had happened to her was just that, an accident, and his presence on that day would not have changed anything. He then asked her to forgive him for not being there to help her any longer. Her response to this request was unexpected. She said that she would feel guilty herself if he had given up his life and happiness for her. She said that apologies and forgiveness were not called for.

Through these conversations and interactions with Katie and his parents, John's self-definition as a loyal and responsible family member was preserved, but the meaning of these terms and labels changed considerably. Similarly, taking care of oneself was no longer considered to be "selfish." Just as Katie had to learn how to take care of herself, John's responsibility was to take care of himself. I observed to John and Sara that they were beginning to understand the difference between taking care of someone and caring for someone, and for being responsible for someone and being responsible to someone. Through this process, John's ideal self was modified to some degree, and the discrepancy between his perceived self and ideal self was reduced.

Attention now turned to Sara. The strategy used with Sara was different from the one employed with John. Cognitive restructuring and reframing were used to help John conceptualize himself differently. Little behavioral change toward his parents and Katie was required. For Sara, on the other hand, behavioral intervention was used to produce cognitive changes and modifications in her self-structure.

Therapist: John, I'd like to focus on your concerns about your in-laws, unless you and Sara think that there is something else you would like to deal with at this time.
John: No, that's fine.
Sara: Yes, that's OK.
Therapist: What do you consider to be the difficulty?
John: The problem is not with me. It has more to do with Sara and her parents.
Therapist: In what way?
John: How they treat Sara, and how she reacts to them.
Therapist: What is it about their treatment of Sara that concerns you?
John: They always question her about her health. It seems that that is all they are concerned with.
Therapist: Sara, what are your thoughts about John's observations?
Sara: I think that he is exaggerating. That's not all we talk about.
Therapist: Why don't you discuss this issue and see if you can come up with something concrete to deal with.
John: OK.
Sara: OK.
John: Maybe I am exaggerating a little, but you all spend a lot of time on health issues.
Sara: Well, with two parents and a sister who are health care providers, sometimes there may be an overemphasis on my well-being.
John: It's not only what you all talk about, it's how you behave.
Sara: What do you mean, how I behave?
John: You start to act like a sick kid.
Sara: That's a real put-down and it's not fair.
John: I don't mean it as a put-down. What I mean is that we have spent so much time in counseling dealing with caretaking and sickness, but when you are with your parents, that part of your personality takes over.
Therapist: John, I can see how concerned you are about Sara. I think you might be afraid that the old pattern, the caretaking and illness pattern, might return.
John: Yes, you're right.
Therapist: John, I don't believe that the "sick child" is part of Sara's personality. I think it is a role that Sara has learned to play in her family. Sara, what do you think?
Sara: Maybe you're right. Maybe it's just a role I've learned to play, but it is the only one I know. I've played it with John. I've played it with friends and coworkers. With my sisters.
Therapist: Is it one that you would like to change?
Sara: Yes and no.
Therapist: What do you mean?
Sara: Yes, I'd like to change it, but I don't know how my parents will react to me. The illness and caretaking pattern has been there between us for as long as I can remember.
Therapist: And if that pattern is removed, you don't know what to expect. How will you know that they care?

Sara: Yes. It sounds weird but it's true.

John: Dr. B., Sara's parents care about her. There is no doubt in my mind that they do, even if they have a strange way of showing it.

Therapist: John, I'm sure you're right, but just as you had to find out for yourself whether your parents thought you were disloyal and whether Katie thought that you were partially to blame for her accident, Sara must also find out for herself.

John: I guess you're right. I understand.

Therapist: And finding out can be a scary business.

Sara: Yes, it can.

Therapist: Sara, when you think you are ready, there is an approach to interacting with your family that we might try.

Sara: What's that?

Therapist: You may want to try out a new and different role when you are with them.

Sara: What kind of role?

Therapist: One that doesn't focus on your health. That doesn't mean that you should not discuss health concerns when it is appropriate, but a role that allows your family to see you differently and to treat you differently—more like an adult, even when you are sick.

Sara: How does that work? How do I do that?

Therapist: I have had some success helping people create new roles for themselves by modeling their behavior after people who behave in ways that they admire. How one acts and what one says certainly affects how one is treated by others. We get what we expect in many cases.

John: Like a self-fulfilling prophecy.

Therapist: Yes, exactly. You may be too young to be familiar with the comedian, Rodney Dangerfield—

John: You mean the guy who gets no respect?

Therapist: Yes, that's him.

John: I've seen his act.

Sara: So have I.

Therapist: Well, one of the reasons he didn't get any respect was because he didn't act like he expected it or deserved it. Therefore no one gave it to him.

We telegraph to people, in a variety of ways, how we expect them to treat us. Sara, behaving differently with your family will most likely produce a different outcome—one that may be more satisfying for you and for everyone else.

Sara: But I can't be sure that they will like how I behave.

Therapist: This is true. Families sometimes try to force people back into old familiar, outmoded, and sometimes dysfunctional roles. There is no way to predict how a family will respond.

Sara: Sounds risky.

Therapist: Yes, there is some risk. There is always a risk when we try something new. I like to think of role creation and role enactment as a kind of experiment. Once you have learned a new role, a new way of behaving, you test it out with people and in situations where there is little or no risk. When you feel confident, then you can ease into it with friends and family members. Sort of like slipping in under the radar.

Sara: Yeah, but you still can get shot down.

Therapist: Bad metaphor.

Sara: (Laughs.) I guess I can give it a try.

Therapist: Can I take my foot out of my mouth now?

Sara: I think so.
John: Sure. No problem.

Models chosen for emulation are the raw material from which a new and more achievable ideal self is fashioned. Sara selected a senior partner from the law firm where she was employed to serve as her role model. This woman, a well-respected attorney, was rarely ill. If she was not feeling well, no one ever knew it. Even a broken ankle did not slow her down. When asked about her condition, her reply was "getting better every day." Although Sara had never given it very much thought in the past, when she began to study this woman, she found that others were drawn to her strength. She was not brash or overbearing. She was competent and self-assured, but she also knew how to relax and enjoy herself. Sara noticed that this woman "looked healthy." She was a member of a local health club and worked out several times a week. Sara decided to join the health club and saw her there from time to time. She adopted a similar hairstyle and began to wear more attractive yet still-professional clothes.

Several sessions were spent helping Sara learn how to deflect questions from others about her health and how to minimize conversations about health-related issues with friends and family members. She learned not to initiate any health-related discussions and to respond matter-of-factly and briefly to any questions about her asthma, allergies, and so on. John was a helpful ally throughout this process. He was supportive and encouraging, and this drew the couple closer together—a benefit that neither John nor Sara had anticipated.

In my discussions with Sara and John about role construction and role enactment, no mention was made of possible changes in the self that might ensue from the cognitive restructuring, which is a pivotal component of the role-enactment process. For example, prior to meeting with her parents and sisters, Sara would recite, subvocally, this phrase, which became a mantra for her: "My physical health is only a small part of who I am, and I won't let it or anyone else define me."

As time went by, less time was spent discussing Sara's health when she and John visited her family, and, her parents seemed to be less concerned about this issue. I suggested that in the future, Sara might consider talking to her internist, rather than her family, whenever she had any medical questions. Sara agreed. When treatment was concluded, Sara remarked that the atmosphere in her parents' home when she visited them seemed to have changed. It was "more light" and less "heavy." She felt a different kind of closeness with her father. As she and John were leaving after our last session, I said, "I think that sickly Sara has left us." Sara smiled and said, "I think she may be gone for good."

DISCUSSION

Personal histories are used to identify salient themes in each spouse's personal mythology. The following questions have proven to be very helpful in this regard:

1. What is your first memory?
2. What is your first memory about your family of origin?
3. Who are the people that make up your family?
4. Who is the person you liked most?
5. Who is the person you liked least?
6. Who is the person you were closest to while you were growing up?
7. Who was the person you feared?
8. Who was the person who had the most power in your family?
9. What was the source of that power?
10. How did this person use his or her power?
11. What person "owned you" emotionally?
12. What was the nature of this emotional attachment?
13. What were the family secrets that everyone knew but that could not be discussed openly?
14. How did your family try to appear to the outside world?
15. How do you think your family was actually viewed by the outside world?
16. What role did each person in your family play?
17. How would you describe the way your family functioned as a system or unit?
18. If you had the power to go back in time and reshape the past, what changes would you make in your family, its members, and how they got along?

The complementary dovetailing of personal themes that evolve into conjugal themes in a couple's mythology often manifest themselves in the following ways:

1. Redundant interaction patterns
2. Recurrent topics of concern
3. Repeated resurfacing of intense emotional conflicts
4. In the couple's characteristic affective tone

Once a conjugal theme has been identified, the therapist must try to determine how the couple used the theme collusively for mutual protection and to preserve dyadic stability. Next, the therapist must try to understand how and why this collusive contract broke down, how it was violated, and so on. Finally, the therapist must decide how to proceed with intervention and what therapeutic techniques are deemed to be appropriate for the couple.

John and Sara's case was chosen for illustration because of its simplicity. Personal and conjugal themes were easy to identify and modify, and major structural changes in the self were not required. Post-treatment evaluations showed that both spouses were satisfied with their therapeutic progress. DAS scores showed considerable improvement, and the three areas of concern identified on the SIDCARB measure were resolved satisfactorily. MSEI scores for both John and Sara showed moderate improvement. Most couples who present for treatment, however, show a much more complex picture. Each spouse brings to the marriage an assortment of personal life themes. Some are positive and growth-enhancing. Some are negative, in the sense that they inhibit personal growth and development. These themes evolve into a loosely integrated system of dyadic themes that constitute the couple's mythology. It would be foolhardy to think that one could successfully edit and modify all dysfunctional personal and conjugal themes that couples bring with them when they come to us for help. The therapeutic challenge is to determine how the theme or constellation of themes is related to the presenting problem.

STUDY QUESTIONS

1. In the case example presented in this chapter, a problematic theme in John and Sara's conjugal mythology was identified. Next, a direct intervention was used to help the couple replace this restrictive interactive dynamic with one that was more personally rewarding and relationship-enhancing. A more subtle and strategic approach to theme editing would be to tell the couple a metaphorical story suggesting a more functional alternative to their "caretaking and illness" pattern.
   a. If you were to use this approach, what metaphorical story would you tell John and Sara?
   b. How would you present this story to them?
2. What are some other strategies that you might use to produce positive changes in the self-definitions of Sara and John that would not require direct intergenerational intervention?

Further Assessment Considerations: Primitive Defenses in Borderline and Narcissistic Disorders 9

This chapter addresses primitive defense mechanisms. These defenses are most commonly encountered in individuals who function at what Kernberg (1985) refers to as borderline and narcissistic levels of personality organization. These defensive operations are discussed below.

Denial. This early defense mechanism is used to avoid experiencing feelings, aspects of reality, and memories that are painful and upsetting. If memories are recalled, however, the negative emotions associated with them are not consciously experienced. Denial is often accompanied by fantasies that reinforce it. Such fantasies may sometimes reach delusional proportions. When this occurs, the person behaves in ways that totally disregard the painful reality. For example, I interviewed a man whose wife had divorced him and remarried. Although he would acknowledge the legal end to his marriage, he believed that he and his wife were still married. They were "soul mates forever." This denial of the end of their marriage was kept alive by the fantasy that his ex-wife would eventually return to him. He continued to wear his wedding ring, referred to her as his "wife," and refused to date other women, since he felt that doing so would be an act of infidelity.

Couples often collude in denial in order to protect each other and to avoid re-experiencing painful events in their marriage. Shared screen memories may be used, in place of shared fantasies, to support this denial. A couple who had been married for several years came to see me about their 5-year-old daughter, who was having considerable difficulty adjusting to kindergarten. This couple had married after the wife discovered she was pregnant. The circumstances surrounding the woman's pregnancy were unclear and the true identity of the father was uncertain. While the couple was engaged, the woman had had a "one night stand" one evening after drinking heavily. This was her only "indiscretion," and she denied that this experience could have led to her pregnancy, since she was certain that she had been unable to conceive during that part of her menstrual cycle. Her fiancé "forgave" her and accepted that he was the father of the child. Neither spouse considered it necessary to undergo paternity testing. Both agreed that the child was his.

Projection. Projection is a common defense mechanism used by the ego to protect the self. In its mildest form, it can be observed in most people. The basic mechanism operating in projection is the unconscious attribution to others of one's own thoughts, feelings, traits, attributes, motives, and desires—things that are unacceptable to consciousness and, therefore, are disavowed and disclaimed. Primitive projection, which is characteristic of borderline and narcissistic personality disorders, differs quantitatively and qualitatively from the sort of projection seen in the general population. In borderline individuals, a split object or a split self, which contains all negative or all positive qualities, is projected onto another. In narcissistic personality disorders, whole and intact idealized or devalued objects and selves are projected. In both conditions, reality testing is severely compromised.

Splitting. The process of keeping separate the good self and good object introjects from the bad self and bad object introjects is referred to as splitting. This is done in order to protect and preserve the good self and good object from contamination and destruction by the bad introjects. Maintaining this separation requires considerable psychic energy, which ordinarily would be available to support other critical ego functions. The result is an overall weakening of the ego, especially in the areas of anxiety management, frustration tolerance, impulse control, ego boundaries, and reality testing. Denial and projection are used to support splitting.

When splitting occurs in marriage, a spouse is sometimes perceived and treated as a projected good object and at other times as a projected bad object. The switch from good object to bad object perceptions may happen suddenly, leaving the targeted spouse upset and confused. I have treated a couple for whom such sudden shifts in perception were common for the wife. The husband referred to his wife's abrupt changes in behavior as her "Jekyll and Hyde personality."

Projective Identification. Projective identification is a complex process that in most cases occurs in rapidly unfolding stages. During the first part of the process, a split-self object is projected onto another person. This split object can be either a good self or a bad self. At the same time, the person doing the projecting becomes identified with the corresponding good or bad parental introject. Next, a role reversal occurs. The person doing the projection treats the projected split self as he or she had been treated by the corresponding parental introject with whom he or she has become identified. If a bad self/bad object projective identification process has taken place, the recipient of the projection will be treated badly. However, if a good self/good object projective identification process has occurred, the recipient of the projection will be treated in an idealized fashion.

In many instances, the recipient of the projection unconsciously accommodates by playing out the assigned reciprocal role of either good self or bad self. This dynamic forms the basis of collusive projective identification, collusive idealization, and collusive negative polarization, as described by Dicks (1967).

For purposes of diagnosis and treatment, it is important to make the distinction between transference and projective identification. In the former case, people are perceived and treated as whole and intact objects. In the latter case, only split objects and split selves are involved in the process. The dynamic of projective identification is easily mistaken for ambivalence. Here again, however, the same distinction applies. The target of ambivalence is usually perceived as a whole intact person, not as a projected split self or split object.

In thinking about projective identification, it is important to remember that disparate and concrete superego forerunners are also part of this complex process. Even in cases where some degree of superego depersonification and abstraction has taken place, the rewarding and protecting aspects of this structure may still remain split off from its critical and punitive components. Since superego integration and consolidation occur late in personality formation, the superego is vulnerable to regression and temporary splitting under unduly stressful conditions and external pressures. It is important to make these distinctions in considering treatment strategies and options.

PRIMITIVE IDEALIZATION AND DEVALUATION

As a shield against projected split objects that are perceived and experienced as all bad, dangerous, destructive, and so on, the person creates a fantasy of a totally good external object that is all-powerful, loving, protecting, and nurturing, with whom he or she can merge and in whose greatness he or she can share. However, when the idealized object fails to live up to the person's fantasized expectations of perfection, which inevitably happens, the object is devalued, demeaned, and demonized.

When this occurs, the once all-good object becomes its all-bad and evil counterpart and is treated accordingly. This dynamic is typical of borderline individuals.

Narcissistic idealization may appear very similar to the idealization of the borderline personality, but it differs in one significant respect. Usually, in narcissism, objects and selves are not split. They retain their integrity. When the therapist is idealized as part of a narcissistic dynamic, the traits and qualities attributed to him or her are usually unfounded, unrealistic, or extreme exaggerations of the therapist's true qualities and attributes. Since projection of the idealized self or object onto the therapist is a central dynamic in narcissism, the traits, qualities, and attributes assigned to the therapist will be linked in some way to the person's own grandiosity. Such projections usually make the therapist feel uncomfortable or uneasy. *Bizarre* or *uncanny*, however, are the adjectives that best describe how one might feel when he or she is the target of idealization by a person with a borderline personality disorder. Whereas the narcissist is detached from the therapist, the borderline personality exhibits a desperate and clinging neediness. Unlike the disconnection one experiences in relation to a person with a narcissistic disorder, the connection with the borderline type is usually intense. Reactions to disillusionment and disappointment are also different for these two conditions. For people in the narcissistic group, disillusionment and disappointment will lead to devaluation and termination of the relationship (unless the relationship is perceived to be nonvoluntary). For the borderline group, however, disillusionment and disappointment lead to demonization, attacks, and, in some cases, the loss of reality testing, transient psychotic symptoms, violence, and self-injurious behavior but not necessarily termination of the relationship, since fear of abandonment plays such a significant role in these individuals' dynamics. Idealization in the borderline group also differs qualitatively from narcissistic idealization in that it is more primitive in terms of its developmental antecedents. Fantasized fusion with one who is idealized in narcissism is a defense against shame, incompetence, and unworthiness. In borderline pathology, fusion with the good split object is often terror-driven. The fear is one of abandonment, destruction, and annihilation. Whereas narcissists struggle with envy, borderline personalities struggle with aggression and their violent urges. Both borderline and narcissistic personality-disordered individuals use ingratiation in their interpersonal dealings, but their motives are different. The narcissist wants to share in the idealized person's power, thereby elevating his or her own self-esteem. The borderline individual, on the other hand, uses ingratiation as an act of supplication that is used to ward off anticipated attacks or abandonment by an all-powerful projected split object. Individuals with narcissistic personality disorders frequently enter therapy in order to heal and repair narcissistic wounds that they have received from spouses, partners, or significant others. Feelings of a bandonment, depression, disruptions to the self, suicidal thoughts, and the emergence of transient psychotic symptoms are usually what cause borderline individuals to seek professional assistance.

Another important distinction that must be made is that between idealization and flattery when these occur in a therapeutic context. Flattery, for the most part, is a conscious manipulative strategy used as a defense. When it is used by one spouse, it is usually designed to seduce the therapist into forming a coalition with that spouse against the other. When used by both spouses, it becomes a collusive defense against meaningful change in the couple's relationship. Idealization, on the other hand, is not a conscious or premeditated attempt to co-opt or neutralize the therapist. For borderline individuals, the goal is to maintain the separation between the good self/good object and the bad self/bad object, so that the latter does not contaminate or destroy the former. The underlying unconscious fantasy is that the idealized all-good therapist and good self (or couple, as the case may be) are joined in a secure cocoon that will serve as a bulwark against destruction. In narcissistic disorders, the self is not divided but rather is inflated and grandiose. In order to maintain this unconscious fantasy of being special, superior, entitled, and so on, narcissistic individuals can associate themselves only with extraordinary people in whose greatness they can share by association. Therefore, the therapist must also be endowed with exceptional qualities, skills, and talents.

Grandiosity and Omnipotence. The belief that the self is special, great, entitled, all-powerful, and in possession of extraordinary skills, gifts, talents, abilities, and so forth is often seen in individuals diagnosed as narcissistic. These defenses are used to combat feelings of incompetence, unworthiness, inadequacy, and inferiority. In order to maintain these feelings and beliefs of one's superiority, devaluation of others is essential. Earlier it was proposed that for marriages to endure without serious conflicts, both spouses must respect and support the defensive operations that their partners have erected to protect and validate the self and to maintain self-esteem. In cases where grandiosity and omnipotence are used, it is essential for the partner to collude by validating this inflated self-concept. If a spouse fails to do so, he or she runs the risk of being devalued and becoming the target of the rage that follows such narcissistic wounding.

It is not unusual to find individuals married to such narcissistic spouses to complain that they have become tired, burned out, or exhausted by their attempts to meet their spouse's constant needs for praise, admiration, adulation, attention, and so on. One wife put it very succinctly: "I'm tired of being his cheerleader."

In relationships where grandiosity and omnipotence are used by both partners, the quid pro quo collusive agreement between the two is fairly simple: "I'll support your grandiosity if you support my grandiosity." Sometimes, both partners share the same grandiose fantasy. Whether such a collusive arrangement can be considered a *folie à deux* depends upon the degree of reality distortion that is required to maintain the fantasy.

The use of primitive defense mechanisms to maintain personal integrity and dyadic stability is a good indication that the self is fragile and self-esteem tenuous. Identification of these defenses during the assessment stage of treatment, therefore, is essential if one is to help couples formulate viable and attainable treatment goals. Treatment of couples where one or both of the partners suffers from a borderline or narcissistic personality disorder is best thought of as a management approach where the number of crises is reduced, conflicts do not escalate out of control, and more satisfying contracts are negotiated.

Working With Primitive Defenses in Couple Therapy: Case Examples of Borderline and Narcissistic Dynamics 10

This chapter is devoted to working with primitive collusive defensive systems that typically characterize relationships in which one or both partners is diagnosed as having a borderline or narcissistic personality disorder. Frequently, individuals form intimate relationships with and marry partners who function at similar levels of personality organization/disorganization. Therefore, one should not be surprised to find that sometimes both partners who present for therapy have diagnosable personality disorders. Given the short-term, problem-focused model of intervention presented in this volume, structural changes in personality organization are not to be expected. The major goals of treatment with this population are as follows:

1. Improved dyadic functioning in the areas of couple communication, problem solving, conflict negotiation, empathy, and role taking
2. Modification of dysfunctional contractual arrangements that are damaging the partners' selves and stifling to the relationship's positive development
3. The strengthening of those contractual agreements that encourage individual growth and enhanced relationship functioning

These goals are not substantially different from those one strives to achieve with most couples that enter marital or relationship therapies. However, with this population, attaining these desired outcomes is always a challenge, and one should not be discouraged by gains that are only modest.

MODIFICATION OF THE ASSESSMENT PROCESS

As mentioned earlier, personal and relationship history interviews allow one to arrive at a diagnosis. If it is determined that one or both of the spouses has a borderline or narcissistic condition, some modification in the assessment process might be in order. For example, since borderline and narcissistic individuals are highly vulnerable and sensitive to criticism, asking them to work through a lengthy, detailed inventory of their relationship may be personally threatening, and threatening to the fragile stability of the marriage. In such cases, it may be appropriate to ask the couple to complete only one or two selected assessment instruments. By limiting the number of assessments, the spouses will tend to see their therapeutic work as clearly defined and manageable.

A NOTE ABOUT SIDCARB

If SIDCARB is selected as a measure to be used in lieu of the full battery of assessment instruments, it is important to keep in mind that Factors II and III measure barrier strengths according to social exchange principles. However, they do not deal with some impediments to relationship termination that are particularly relevant for borderline and narcissistic individuals, such as fears of being abandoned, alone, and isolated, or the conviction that no one else would want to marry or be with such a damaged, disgusting, bad, or evil person. SIDCARB barrier score question 26 asks respondents to list any additional considerations (not included in the questionnaire) that might prevent them from terminating an unsatisfying marriage. Sometimes, fears of abandonment and beliefs about one's own worthiness are cited, but such issues are rarely mentioned. For the most part, this information is usually disclosed in the privacy of individual assessment interviews and not included in the SIDCARB, since these comments will be read by the spouse.

Sometimes, borderline or narcissistic partners become threatened by assessment once it gets under way because they interpret the various instruments as measures of pathology (badness), achievement potential, or intelligence. In spite of reassurances to the contrary, these individuals may still be reluctant to complete the process. When this occurs, the Relationship Problem Questionnaire (RPQ) may serve as a less-threatening alternative (see Appendix B). The RPQ can also be used when measures of marital satisfaction, adjustment, and so forth are not appropriate.

THERAPEUTIC STRUCTURE

Borderline and narcissistic individuals often have difficulty keeping hostile, aggressive, and angry impulses under control. If therapy is to progress successfully, a procedure for keeping these destructive impulses in check must be instituted at the outset of treatment. Both partners must be sure that the therapeutic environment is a safe one. In some cases, the therapist's office may be the only place where both spouses feel safe. Structuring the couple's communication-interaction processes is central to the establishment of a safe therapeutic environment. Guidelines for establishing functional communication between spouses (Bagarozzi, 2001) have been modified specifically for work with this population. These guidelines and a discussion of the rationale for the use of them are offered in Appendix C.

BORDERLINE DYNAMICS: PAUL AND TINA

Paul contacted me for an individual appointment. When he came in for his first interview, he was anxious and depressed. He was concerned about his "sex drive." When asked to elaborate, he said that he had lost his desire to have intercourse with his fiancée but was still sexually attracted to other women. He said that he would never act upon these desires. He loved his fiancée, Tina, very much and could not understand what was "wrong with him." He said that he masturbated from time to time, but not frequently, and that his masturbatory fantasies usually involved women other than his fiancée. He had never experienced this problem in any former relationship. Paul, 37, had never been married. Prior to becoming engaged, Paul and Tina had had a fulfilling sexual relationship. It was not until about 3 months after their engagement that this problem began.

I asked Paul if he had any explanations for his lack of desire for Tina, but he could not explain his behavior. He said she was beautiful and sexy and that he "admired and respected" her. Tina was the only woman he had ever considered marrying. Tina had suggested that Paul might be "afraid of commitment," but Paul stated that this was not the case, that he was fully committed to Tina without any reservation.

Relevant Personal History

Paul

Paul was an only child. His parents divorced when he was 3 years old. His mother remarried when he was 6 and was divorced again when Paul was 9. She lived with several men in succession but never remarried. Paul had little respect for his mother and deplored her lifestyle. After graduating from high school, Paul went to live with his father and his father's girlfriend, whom Paul described as "trashy." This woman had a daughter who was a few years older than Paul. Paul said that she "seduced" him and they had a sexual relationship that lasted for about a year, until she left home. Paul attended college but did not complete his degree. He worked for a while in the automobile parts department of a large retail store, then took a position as assistant manager in a hardware store. He worked his way up to a managerial position and then borrowed money to buy his own hardware business. During these years, Paul dated a number of women but did not have any long-term or serious relationships. He was 35 years old when he met Tina. They dated for a year before moving in together.

Tina

Tina was 6 and her brother was 4 when her father deserted the family, He "left for work one morning and never came home again." Her mother was devastated and never fully recovered from the trauma. She became clinically depressed. Tina's maternal grandparents moved into her home in order to care for the family after one of Tina's mother's bouts of depression. Tina considered her grandfather to be her father. He was a loving, kind man who died from a heart attack when Tina was 11. After her grandfather's death, Tina took on the role of parental child, caring for her mother and younger brother. Tina did not have much of a social life in high school. Her major concerns were her mother's emotional health and her brother's well-being. She lived at home while attending college and had no serious romantic relationships until she was in her late twenties. She dated one man exclusively for about a year and a half when she was 26, but he ended the relationship in order to marry another woman. Shortly after this failed relationship, Tina met a man who was considerably older than she. They married and were planning to have children when he was killed in an automobile accident. Tina had a very difficult time getting over the loss of her husband. She said that all the men in her life either "deserted her or died." She was 31 when she met Paul. She described her relationship with Paul as being "very good" until he began to lose interest in her sexually. In all other ways, he remained attentive and considerate of her.

INITIAL COUPLE SESSION

Therapist: Good evening, folks. Come in and have a seat.
Paul: Thank you.

Tina: Nice to meet you. Paul said he had a good visit with you the other night.

Therapist: Yes, I think it was very productive.

Tina: I know Paul told you about our problem, so you know why we are here.

Therapist: Paul has told me about your difficulties from his perspective. Now I'd like to get your perspective.

Tina: We aren't having any sex. We have not had sex in 2 months. Before we got engaged, sex was not a problem. After our engagement, it all went downhill.

Therapist: What have you done to solve this problem in the past?

Tina: We've tried to talk about it, but each time we do it turns into an argument. Paul is very defensive. He feels blamed.

Paul: I know it's my fault. Tina has done nothing wrong, but I just don't have the interest. I hope you can help us.

Tina: What upsets me is that I know Paul has a sex drive. I know he masturbates and sometimes when he gets up in the morning he has an erection. I don't think his problem is physical. I think it is psychological. Maybe he just isn't attracted to me anymore. I have put on a few pounds since we first met.

Paul: No. That's not a factor. I still find you very attractive.

Tina: What is it then?

Paul: I don't know.

Tina: You see, Dr. Bagarozzi, this is how it always goes. We come to this point and we get stuck.

Therapist: Yes, I can see what you mean. You keep going over the same ground again and again.

Tina: Over and over and I'm tired of it.

Paul: It gets old after a while.

Therapist: Very frustrating.

Tina: Very.

DISCUSSION

In the time remaining, Paul and Tina were taught functional communication skills. At the close of the session, Paul and Tina were given their assessment package and individual interviews were scheduled for the following week. When they returned for their assessment feedback session, the couple said that working on their sexual relationship was a priority, even though a number of additional issues had been identified as problematic. I agreed with their assessment of the situation and suggested that the couple begin by using sensate focus exercises in the privacy of their home. I explained the sensate focus format and the rationale for the procedure, then gave them a set of detailed guidelines. Tina and Paul said that since they had rented a cabin in the mountains for the weekend, they would be able to concentrate on this homework assignment without much interference.

Sensate focus exercises have a number of uses. On the surface, they are presented to a couple as a desensitization procedure that is meant to help partners "reconnect physically," gradually, and at their own pace. The nondemanding format of sensate focus reduces performance anxiety. Sensate focus is also a valuable diagnostic tool. How partners respond to this homework assignment reveals a great deal about their relationship, interaction patterns, and possible collusive dynamics. Finally, since the couple is asked to refrain from engaging in sexual intercourse during the first stage of the process, sensate focus acts as a paradoxical strategic restraining technique.

ASSESSMENT PROCESS

Since Paul and Tina were not formally married, traditional measures of marital satisfaction and SIDCARB were not administered. Part I of the Relationship Problems Questionnaire was used in their place. A reworded version of the Marital Disaffection Scale (MDS) was also administered. In all questions, the term *partner* replaced the word *spouse*. In addition to the Intimacy Needs Questionnaire and Images, the Sexual Desire Inventory (Spector, Carey, & Steinberg, 1996) was also included. This instrument is helpful in assessing whether each partner's sexual needs are being met in his or her relationship with a significant other. It is also a good measure of hypoactive sexual desire. This 14-item instrument comprises two empirically derived factors: dyadic sexual desire and solitary sexual desire. It helps the therapist determine whether the problem is a more general one or specific to the particular partner.

Relationship Problems Questionnaire

General satisfaction scores on the RPQ were in the low range for Tina. The following relationship satisfaction scores were scored as "not at all satisfied": intimacy, communication, sexual relations, and leisure time. Paul identified these same four dimensions of the relationship as "not at all satisfied."

Intimacy Needs Questionnaire

Paul's total intimacy needs strength score was considered to be low (414). Tina's score was within the average range (572). Paul indicated receptivity and reciprocity dissatisfaction in the area of sexual intimacy, even though his sexual desire for Tina was "blocked." He also indicated reciprocity dissatisfaction for emotional, psychological, and intellectual intimacy. Tina indicated that sexual intimacy and emotional intimacy were problematic for her. Both receptivity and reciprocity were seen as falling below acceptable levels.

Trust Scale

Trust scores are reported in percentages: the higher the percentage, the higher the trust for each factor. The following percentage scores were computed for Paul's level of trust of Tina: faith 69%, dependability 94%, and predictability 66%. Tina's rating of Paul on this measure was considerably lower: faith 51%, dependability 48%, and predictability 51%.

Images

Discrepancy scores (D scores), which are also reported as percentages, were not particularly high for the couple. D = 13% for Paul and D = 21% for Tina.

Disaffection

Tina's Disaffection score was 57 and Paul's was 40. These numbers show that Tina's emotional investment in the relationship was decidedly less than Paul's.

Sexual Desire Inventory

This scale consists of 14 items. Scores assessing sexual desire for one's partner range from 0 to 54. Scores assessing sexual desire for someone other than one's partner range from 0 to 16. Scores measuring the strength of solitary sexual desire and behavior range from 0 to 40. Tina reported high scores for all three subscales. Paul reported low scores for sex with Tina and a moderate score for sex with a different partner. Solitary sexual desire, however, was high.

SENSATE FOCUS ASSESSMENT

The sensate focus homework assignment proved to be a valuable assessment tool, which shed some light upon a number of significant personal and couple dynamics. Excerpts from the session after the couple returned from their weekend stay in the mountains are presented below.

Therapist: Good evening.
Paul: Good evening.
Tina: Nice to see you.
Paul: We did not do our homework.
Tina: It was a disaster.
Therapist: Tell me. What went wrong?
Tina: When we arrived at the cabin on Friday evening, Paul said that he was too tired to do any sensate focus exercises after driving all day. We went out for dinner. At the restaurant, we met another couple. Paul struck up a friendship with the husband and the two men made plans to go trout fishing on Saturday. The man's wife, Kelly, and I decided that we would go shopping in the town while Paul and her husband were fishing. Paul and Jack, that's his name, said they would meet us later in the afternoon at the lake. Paul and Jack arrived about two or three o'clock in the afternoon. We left the beach about five in the evening. *Paul and I had planned to do our homework that night before we went to sleep, so after dinner we both took showers, like the guidelines suggest, and went into the bedroom. That's when it all fell apart.*
Therapist: What happened?
Paul: I could not go through with it. I got very nervous and panicked. Both of us being naked and all that. I just could not do it. I felt very uncomfortable. I felt closed in. Tina got very mad, and I can't blame her.
Therapist: Tina, I suspect you were also hurt. I'm sure it was frustrating for both of you.
Tina: At first I was mad. Now, I'm just discouraged.
Therapist: Maybe it was premature to assign sensate focus for your first homework assignment.
Tina: What do you mean?
Therapist: Perhaps it was too much, too soon. Maybe my timing was off.
Tina: I don't think so. I think it is about time we tried something to get us started.
Therapist: Well, people move at their own pace. Perhaps both of you may not be ready at this time. When you are both ready you both will know. There are some things that you just can't rush, and this may be one of them.
Tina: I think I'm more than ready!
Paul: Maybe you're right. Maybe I'm not ready yet.
Therapist: Take your time. Don't pressure yourselves. When the time is right, you'll know.
Tina: Well, that's not the only problem we had last weekend. There's more.
Therapist: What else happened?
Tina: When we were driving home on Sunday afternoon, Paul asked me if I had had sex with Kelly while he and Jack were trout fishing. I don't know where in the world Paul got such a crazy idea. He knows that I am a faithful and honest person. I've never been unfaithful to anyone in my life, and he knows that I am one hundred percent heterosexual.
Therapist: Paul, what made you suspect that Tina might have had sex with Kelly?
Paul: Maybe, since I don't have sex with her, she'll get it somewhere else. Kelly is a very attractive woman. She looks like one of those Victoria's Secret models. Jack told me that she is an uninhibited sex partner.

Tina: Dr. Bagarozzi, I think that Paul feels guilty because he was sexually attracted to Kelly. That's what I think.

Therapist: Paul, do you think that you might have been attributing some of your feelings about Kelly to Tina?

Paul: I don't know. If I did, it was not conscious.

Therapist: That's usually how it works. Thoughts and feelings that may be consciously unacceptable to us are sometimes attributed to others.

Paul: Kelly is certainly a good-looking woman. She reminds me of one of those women who can really enjoy down and dirty sex.

Therapist: "Down and dirty." That's an interesting way of putting it.

Tina: Paul, we used to have "down and dirty" sex when we first hooked up. I liked "down and dirty." It was good. It was fun. Then it turned into "down and out." Now, it's "completely out."

Therapist: Paul, sometimes some people find it difficult to be tender, loving, and caring with a person and still be sexual with that person. In other cases, if sex is considered to be bad, dirty, or sinful, one may not be able to accept a partner who is seen as good as also being sexual. You know. There are "good girls" and "bad girls," and this distinction will certainly affect one's relationships. Do you think this might be playing a part in your feelings toward Tina?

Paul: Maybe there is something to that theory. It sounds possible.

Therapist: You've said that you "admire" and "respect" Tina.

Paul: Yes, she is one of the few women that I admire and respect.

Therapist: I wonder if you can't have "down and dirty" sex with someone you admire and respect. Perhaps, once you decided to marry Tina, she became a "good girl," and maybe you don't want to make her a dirty, bad girl.

Paul: Well, if that's the case, it must be all unconscious.

Tina: I think you hit on something. It's like a switch was flipped after we got engaged. Paul showed more interest in *Playboy* magazine than he did in me.

DISCUSSION

Paul and Tina's failure to complete their sensate focus homework may represent a collusive defense that the couple used to resist the therapist's attempt to impose his rules for power sharing and exchange on the couple's relationship and to distract the therapist from focusing upon more profound personal and relationship problems. In this sense, the presenting problem for which the couple sought treatment served as a smokescreen that masked the partners' struggles for dominance and control and Paul's use of psychiatric symptoms to gain a superior complementary position in the couple's relationship.

The temptation might be to concentrate on the sensate focus assignment—that is, exploring the reasons for noncompliance, modifying the homework, and reassigning the task. If this course were chosen, the diversion would probably be successful. Another pitfall would be to see Paul as being at fault for the couple's inability to complete the assignment and sympathetically siding with Tina against him.

By assuming responsibility for Paul and Tina's failure to complete the sensate focus homework and divesting himself of personal interest in the successful outcome of the assignment, the therapist avoided being triangulated and pulled into a power struggle with the couple. Similarly, by discussing the failed assignment in terms of the couple not being ready (as opposed to Paul not being ready) to make a change, therapeutic neutrality was underscored.

Noncompliance was dealt with strategically by using a restraining technique followed by a cryptic indirection about the couple's readiness to know when "the time is right." These techniques are often helpful with severely distressed systems at the beginning stages of therapy (Watzlawick, Weakland, & Fisch, 1974; Weeks & L'Abate, 1982).

Under most circumstances, projection that reaches delusional proportions is not usually addressed early in the therapeutic process. Such interpretations are reserved for later in the treatment, when trust has been established, but Tina's insightful comments could not be ignored. They were addressed but not dwelt upon. However, the groundwork had been laid for revisiting this defense at a later time. Similarly, interpretations of defensive splitting are usually postponed until there is a solid foundation of therapeutic trust, but Paul's comments about "down and dirty sex" opened the door. Here again, this defensive process was not overemphasized. Splitting was simply described as a possible explanation for Paul's behavior and was not pursued any further.

Conflicts over closeness and separateness—that is, intimacy—are particularly acute in relationships where there is borderline pathology. The basic human need for intimacy (Bagarozzi, 2001) drives a person to pursue closeness with another individual, but too much closeness is frightening and, in some cases, too much closeness may be terrifying, leading to fears of engulfment, of losing control, of loss of identity, and that one's bad or evil self will be discovered when a relationship becomes too intimate. Such fears cause the person to distance himself or herself. However, too much distance and prolonged separation can often cause one to feel a self-imposed rejection and abandonment. The need for intimacy and the fear of intimacy often manifest themselves in a seesaw, back and forth, pursuer-distancer interaction that is characteristic of borderline dynamics. In this case, the use of restraining gave Paul and Tina permission to distance themselves temporarily without feeling judged or accused by the therapist.

Total intimacy needs strength scores in the 400 range are low but not uncommon. A component needs strengths analysis of Paul's scores showed that low scores were characteristic in all eight component domains. His sexual needs strength score was 36/100, which is extremely low. Tina's score for this component need was 90/100. Such differing scores are usually indicative of a desire discrepancy. A desire discrepancy may not be evident during the dating and courtship period, since the low-desire partner's sexual behavior may be more situationally determined than reflective of his or her true need. This problem is exacerbated when the low-desire partner has a borderline personality and is pressed to be more sexually involved than he or she is capable of being. Avoidance of sexual relations can be seen as a manifestation of a more pervasive fear of intimacy.

During the assessment feedback session, Paul and Tina were made aware of their needs strengths differences in the area of sexual intimacy. However, these differences were not described as a "desire discrepancy," since doing so might only have conveyed the idea that nothing could be done to ameliorate the problem. Their differences were simply portrayed as one of the important areas of intimacy in need of attention.

THE COURSE OF TREATMENT

The use of restraint alleviated some of the pressure to solve the sexual problem immediately. I suggested that the couple consider addressing those areas of their relationship where they might be able to achieve greater levels of intimacy while the sexual issue was "put on the back burner for a while." Paul and Tina agreed that a "temporary break" might be helpful.

Therapist: As I was reviewing your Intimacy Needs Questionnaires earlier today, I noticed that there are three other areas where there are intimacy concerns. If there is nothing else that you would like to focus on today, I think the Intimacy Needs Questionnaire would be a good place to start.

Tina: That's OK.

Paul: Fine.

Therapist: The three other areas of intimacy are emotional, psychological, and intellectual intimacy. How would you like to approach these areas?

Paul: In all three of these areas, reciprocity satisfaction with Tina is very low. I'd like to start there.

Therapist: OK. Use the communication skills you have learned to discuss this issue. I'll get into my coach/teacher role and help you out if you need some help.

Paul: Tina, you never share any of your thoughts and feelings with me in these areas.

Tina: How do you expect me to respond when you always criticize me for disagreeing with you? It's better for me not to say anything.

Therapist: Let's stop for a minute to review the speaker's and listener's guidelines. (Gives couple another set of guidelines to review.) Try not to blame each other or talk in absolutes. You know "never," "always." Speak from the "I" position. Now, let's start again.

Paul: You say that I criticize you for disagreeing with me, but I am not criticizing. I just like to have a lively debate.

Tina: You say you like to have a debate, but it feels like criticism.

Therapist: Tina, you experience Paul's debating style as criticism. That's your interpretation. That's your perception of his behavior.

Tina: Yes, that's how it feels.

Therapist: And you respond to Paul by not saying anything.

Tina: Yes, I withdraw mostly. Sometimes I blow up and cuss him out. I think sometimes he deliberately wants to hurt me, to make me feel small and stupid.

Therapist: Paul, some people get energized by a lively debate, and some people use debating as a way to connect with others. I'm curious about how you learned to debate. When did you first start to debate with people?

Paul: One of my mother's boyfriends used to debate with me. His name was Fred. He said that he wanted me to think logically, so if I had an opinion, he challenged me to be logical.

Therapist: Do you remember how it felt to debate with Fred?

Paul: Sometimes it got pretty heated. At ten or eleven years old, I did not have all the facts. Mainly I just had my opinions.

Therapist: How did you feel about that?

Paul: Sometimes I felt dumb.

Therapist: And angry, too, I suspect.

Paul: Yes, sometimes angry.

Therapist: Sometimes, when we are frightened, especially when we are little, we behave like the person who frightens us. It gives us a sense of control—even a sense of power.

Tina: That makes sense.

Therapist: I suggest that the next time you find yourselves in a debate that you stop and use these communication skills. Maybe this will make it easier for Tina to reciprocate—share her thoughts and feelings with you, Paul.

DISCUSSION

In the first set of exchanges, a potential symmetrical escalation of the couple's conflict was averted by asking Paul and Tina to employ the communication skills they had learned earlier. It is important to interrupt negative reciprocity as soon as it begins in order to maintain the security and safety of the therapeutic environment and to prevent a return to destructive and dysfunctional patterns of communication. Whenever possible, the couple is addressed as a unit; for example, "Try not to blame each other or talk in absolutes." This allows the therapist to maintain therapeutic neutrality.

In the next set of exchanges, two defenses are highlighted: projective identification and identification with the aggressor. These defenses are not labeled as problematic. They are described as possible ways that one might use to deal with upsetting or frightening experiences. Here again, the therapist's comments are not presented as psychological interpretations. They are offered in passing, as simple observations.

Paul and Tina continued to discuss their concerns having to do with emotional, psychological, and intellectual intimacy for three weeks. In the fourth week, Paul began the session by saying:

Paul: Doc, we have some good news and some bad news to talk about today.

Therapist: Where would you like to start, with the good news or the bad news?

Paul: The good news is that we had sex last weekend, and we had some good talks. We used the communication guidelines, sort of, and we had some good discussions, but we did not do the sensate focus homework.

Therapist: Sounds like you are making progress.

Tina: The bad news is that we had a fight on Monday.

Therapist: Let's review what happened and let's see if you can work out the problem during this session.

Tina: We had sex Sunday evening. It wasn't planned or anything. It just happened spontaneously, and that was really good.

Paul: Yes, it was good.

Tina: This is what I don't understand. Paul says that the sex was good, but Monday I caught him masturbating in the shower. If it was so good, why didn't he approach me again?

Therapist: Paul, what are your thoughts and feelings about this incident?

Paul: I don't know. I just felt I needed to.

Tina: But you knew I would see you. You left the shower door open. I think you did it just to hurt me.

Paul: I did not do it to hurt you.

Tina: I really don't understand. Dr. Bagarozzi, do you have any idea what is going on with us?

Therapist: Sometimes people need some distance after being close and intimate. Having a fight is one way to get that distance, but it still keeps people connected in a passionate but negative way.

Tina: There has got to be a better way of doing that. Getting that distance, I mean.

Therapist: Talking about your fears of being close can be helpful in this regard. Would you like to explore them today?

Tina: I would.

Therapist: Paul, would you like to focus on this issue today?

Paul: Not really, but I guess we should.

Therapist: We can wait until both of you are ready. There is no need to force the issue now.

Paul: No. Let's go ahead.

Therapist: You said that over the weekend you had had some good discussions. I wonder if something was said during one of your discussions that made you feel uncomfortable?

Tina: We did talk about a few things that were upsetting—

Paul: I don't want to talk about them here. Let's just say that they are things I'm not proud of.

Therapist: Paul, I respect your right to privacy. There is no need to talk about them here.

Paul: Maybe some other time, but not now.

Therapist: I understand. If you want to bring up these issues, I'll be glad to discuss them with you whenever you feel the need.

Paul: Thanks, Doc.

Tina: Dr. Bagarozzi, I feel honored that Paul trusts me enough to share these things with me, but if he trusts me so much, why would he want to put some distance between us?

Therapist: Paul, can you help Tina out? Can you help her understand what is going on?

Paul: Tina, I don't understand why you want to be with me when I have been such a bad person.

Tina: Paul, you've done some bad things, but that does not make you a bad person. What you did happened years ago.

Paul: But I still feel guilty and ashamed of myself.

Therapist: Paul, when you feel this way, I think it is hard for you to experience the good parts of yourself. The good parts may be walled off for protection.

Paul: Sometimes I'm not sure there are any good parts of me.

Therapist: Maybe when you distance yourself from Tina, you are also trying to protect her from those negative parts of yourself. Especially, the dirty sexual parts.

Paul: I push her away, you mean?

Therapist: I think that may be so. You may be doing that for her own protection.

Tina: I think you are trying to test me.

Paul: What do you mean, test you?

Tina: To see if I love you.

Therapist: I think Tina might mean that you may be trying to find out just how bad you can be before she rejects you. You have said that you are totally committed to Tina, but maybe you are not sure that she is totally committed to you.

Tina: I am totally committed to you, Paul. I would not reject you. I know very well what it feels like to be rejected and abandoned, and I would never do that to you. You know, and we have discussed this before, there only two deal breakers in our relationship: if you were abusive or unfaithful.

Paul: I know those are deal breakers.

Therapist: There may be another part of this test.

Tina: What is that?

Therapist: To see if you will use what Paul has told you about himself to hurt him when you are angry with him—to use what you know about Paul against him to gain the upper hand in an argument.

Tina: I would never do that to you, Paul.

Paul: Maybe I have been testing you.

Tina: Maybe it is time to stop now.

Paul: Maybe so.

DISCUSSION

The possibility of being scapegoated and triangulated must always be taken into account when borderline dynamics are present. Sensitivity to criticism is central to this condition; therefore, I did not respond in any way that might have been interpreted as disapproving when Paul and Tina revealed that they had failed to follow sensate focus guidelines before engaging in sexual intercourse. Similarly, I did not show any surprise or approval when they reported having had sexual relations. I simply acknowledged their progress and moved on. Although praise for a couple's achievements may be considered positively reinforcing, the therapist's failure to praise the couple, later in treatment, may then be interpreted as criticism. The absence of positive reinforcement may be experienced as punishment. Suffice it to say that the restraining strategies were successful.

Splitting is used to keep the good self and good object separate from the bad self and bad object. The fear here is that the former will be contaminated or destroyed by the latter. Paul is struggling with two issues. He is trying to keep his good self and his bad self apart, and he is trying to protect Tina (whom he sees as a projected idealized good object) from contamination by the bad projected object. At the same time, he is trying to protect the idealized, good Tina from his bad self. These are the dynamics that are first targeted for discussion. *There is no expectation that such interpretations will bring about an integration of objects or selves.* The purpose of these interpretations is to convey empathic understanding. It allows the couple to make some sense out of what was once perceived as incomprehensible (crazy) behavior.

Trust is central to work with all couples, but it takes on added significance in borderline pathology where suspiciousness and paranoid thinking are often part of the clinical picture. In the introduction to this volume, I stressed the importance of partners' nonverbalized contractual agreements not to attack each other's vulnerable selves. I used Tina's statements about trust to make this agreement an openly acknowledged clause in this couple's relationship contract. Finally, trust was used as an opening for discussing rejection and abandonment. Paul's commitment to Tina and her commitment to him were affirmed and grounds for relationship termination were stipulated. Since the fear of rejection and abandonment are central to borderline dynamics, the importance of having Tina and Paul discuss these issues in contractual form cannot be overstated.

Throughout the course of treatment the therapist should expect primitive defenses and borderline dynamics to resurface from time to time. Devising interventions that will reduce the negative effects of these defensive processes makes work with this population challenging.

NARCISSISTIC PERSONALITY DISORDERS: BASIC DYNAMICS

Before proceeding with the following case study, a review of the central features characteristic of narcissistic personality disorders, as outlined in the *Diagnostic and*

Statistical Manual of Mental Disorders (DSM-IV-TR) of the American Psychiatric Association, is presented.

Diagnostic Criteria

The hallmark of narcissistic pathology is a pervasive pattern of grandiosity, need for admiration, and lack of empathy that begins in early adulthood and is present a variety of interpersonal contexts.

Individuals with this condition have a grandiose sense of self-importance; they exaggerate their achievements and talents and expect to be recognized as superior without commensurate accomplishment. They often assume that others attribute the same value to their achievements and may be surprised when the praise they expect and believe they deserve is not forthcoming. This sense of self-importance is accompanied by an underestimation and devaluation of the contributions of others.

There is a preoccupation with fantasies of unlimited success, power, intelligence, beauty, and ideal love. Individuals with this disorder are often obsessed with becoming famous and admired by others. They envision themselves as being elite and deserving of privilege.

Individuals with a narcissistic personality disorder believe that they are special, unique, and superior to others, and they expect everyone to recognize them as such. They will associate only with people they believe to be special, gifted, unique, talented, perfect, and of high status. Their own sense of self-esteem, competence, and worth is enhanced by their associations with those whom they have come to idealize. When they are disappointed by these idealized associates, for whatever reason, these same individuals are then devalued and demeaned.

In narcissists, it is common to note a sense of entitlement and a lack of sensitivity to the wants and needs of others. When they do recognize the needs and feelings of others, these are viewed disparagingly as indicative of weakness, vulnerability, and incompetence.

Envy is a major force in the lives of narcissistic individuals. They begrudge the successes of others and covet their possessions, but they want others to envy them.

Narcissistic individuals are extremely sensitive to criticism and perceived slights. Reactions to criticism can take a variety of forms, ranging from mild irritation and sadness to intense rage and depression.

Narcissism and Self-Esteem

In Chapter 1, self-esteem was shown to be made up of two interrelated factors: worthiness and competence (Mruk, 1995). High levels of competence and worthiness are associated with high self-esteem, whereas low levels of competence and worthiness are associated with low self-esteem. When competence is low but one's sense of self-worth is high, benign forms of narcissism develop as a defense against feelings of incompetence. However, when one is competent and effective but does not feel worthy and loved, more pathological forms of defensive narcissism may develop that are characteristic of what Kernberg (1985) refers to as the "malignant narcissism" of an antisocial personality disorder. In my experience, the line separating benign forms of narcissism from those of the malignant type is not so clearly defined. This distinction is a theoretical one, based upon a categorical view of psychiatric diagnoses. I have found a dimensional approach that takes into account the severity of each symptom to be more clinically useful than a categorical one for planning interventions and structuring treatments with this population.

NARCISSISTIC DYNAMICS: ALLAN AND MARY

This couple was referred for marriage counseling by the priest who had married them 2 years earlier. Allan and Mary had gone to her for pastoral guidance in the past. This time, however, she thought it would be appropriate to refer them for more "in-depth counseling." The couple had given her permission to talk with me about their difficulties, so I had some information about their relationship prior to meeting with them for the first time. Their pastor was concerned that the couple seemed to be "drifting through life with no definite plan."

Mary came from a prominent, well-respected family. She had been "sheltered" and "protected" by her parents and her two older brothers all her life. She attended private schools from kindergarten through college and had always worked in the family's business. Academics were difficult for her. Mary's graduation from a small liberal arts college was a source of pride and relief to her parents. She dated infrequently and did not consider herself to be an attractive woman. Her parents had ambivalent feelings about her marriage to Allan. Although they were happy that Mary was married, they had some misgivings about Allan.

Mary and Allan had both been members of their church choir when they met. Allan also served as lector from time to time, and Mary was very impressed with his knowledge of the scriptures. After choir practice, the two occasionally went out for coffee together. This soon became a regular practice, and subsequently Allan, 27, and Mary, 22, began to date exclusively. Little was known about Allan's past other than he had left his home in California soon after receiving his master's degree from the University of California at Berkeley.

Initial Interview

Allan and Mary arrived 15 minutes early for their first appointment. Both were anxious. Allan said that he and Mary became "worried" when their pastor recommended that they call me for help. They did not think that their problems were "that serious." I responded by saying that it was my understanding that most pastoral counseling is quite brief, two or three sessions, and that referrals are made when the priest believes that further counseling is needed. I added that this should not be construed as meaning that the couple's problems were necessarily very serious. It simply meant that a little more time may be required to solve them than their pastor was able to offer. This seemed to put the couple at ease. Mary responded to my request that they describe what they believed to be the problem.

Mary: Doctor, we have a good marriage and we really love each other. There is nothing wrong with our marriage. It is our circumstances that are the problem.

Therapist: What are the circumstances?

Mary: I'd like to give you some background if that is OK with you.

Therapist: Yes, history is always important for understanding current problems.

Mary: Yes, I know, you told me that over the phone when I called for an appointment.

Therapist: OK. Where would you like to begin?

Mary: Allan is a writer, but he has been unable to get anything published. I think he is a good writer, but his short stories have been turned down by a number of magazines and that has been discouraging.

Therapist: Allan, I'm sorry to hear that. This must be very disappointing for you.

Allan: Not really. Many famous writers have had a lot of rejections before they finally made it.

Mary: Allan is very optimistic. That is one of the things that attracted me to him—his optimism. I'm more discouraged that Allan is. He is sure that his talents will be recognized eventually, but, in the meantime, our finances are not so good, and that is frustrating.

Therapist: What have you done to address your financial difficulties?

Mary: I work in my family's business, and that pays the bills, but things are pretty tight.

Allan: I'm working on a new short story. I think this one is going to be received well.

Mary: I've suggested that Allan try to teach at the community college. He's got a master's degree in English literature, but Allan doesn't like teaching.

Allan: I just can't see myself going in to a class of community college students who are barely literate and correcting their English. They get most of their ideas from Wikipedia, anyway. Not an original thought in their heads.

Therapist: I can see how that would be frustrating and unrewarding.

Allan: Teaching is not for me. I don't have time to plan lessons and review homework assignments.

Mary: It is a little embarrassing at times when my family ask about Allan. They ask if he has gotten anything published or if he has, at least, gotten a part-time job. My parents have even offered to give him a job, but Allan won't hear of it.

Allan: I will not work in a department store.

Mary: Doctor, Allan thinks that working in my parents' business, even part-time, would mean that he is a failure. I don't think so, and it would only be temporary.

Allan: You knew I was a writer when you met me. I remember you thought it was exciting and romantic. Isn't that right, Mary?

Mary: Yes, that's true, but you were working at the time, and I thought you would continue to work after we got married.

Allan: I was not going to work in a bookstore for the rest of my life. Once we got married, I was able to devote all my time to my writing.

Therapist: It seems that you both made some assumptions about what life would be like after marriage—at least as far as working was concerned.

Mary: Doctor, I think that's a fair thing to say. I guess it is mostly my fault. I never had to worry about money. I just assumed that Allan would continue working.

Allan: But I told you, Mary, that after we were married I would have a lot more time for my writing, didn't I?

Mary: Yes, you did, buy you did not say you would leave your job. That came as a surprise to me.

Allan: Mary, you don't have any faith in me.

Mary: That's not at all true. I think you are very talented, and I know you will be a success someday. I'm just frustrated, and you know I want to have a family.

Allan: Well, that will have to wait. You know we can't even think of starting a family now. I have to get established before we have children.

Mary: You're right. I guess I'm being selfish.

DISCUSSION

Mary and Allan's case is another example of the presenting problem being used as a collusive defense. Mary acts as the spokesperson for the couple. Her opening statements exemplify collusive denial and externalization, but the spouses' anxiety betrays their fear that the therapist might discover that there are also more serious relationship problems in their marriage. As the session progresses, however, Mary's concerns begin to emerge. Allan's response is also telling. He denies that having his short stories rejected is disappointing, rationalizes this rejection, and protects his self-esteem by identifying with other "famous" authors whose talents were not immediately recognized and appreciated. Mary quickly comes to his aid to salve the narcissistic wounds that these repeated rejections have inflicted by pointing to his optimism and underscoring his talents.

Mary's attempt to help solve the couple's financial difficulties by suggesting that Allan apply for a teaching position at a community college is met with disdain. Allan attacks and devalues the students and makes it clear that such a teaching position is beneath him. Mary finds herself in a difficult position. She must protect Allan's fragile self-esteem and defend her husband to her family when he rejects her parents' offer of help. Allan's anger begins to rise when Mary voices her concern about his decision to stop working shortly after they married. Her questioning of his decision threatens his sense of entitlement. He takes no responsibility for the couple's plight and puts Mary on the defensive by accusing her of having lost faith in him.

Empathic failure prevents Allan from recognizing Mary's feelings about wanting to start a family. Her comments are discounted. In order to deescalate the conflict, Mary takes a submissive, complementary position by accepting responsibility for the couple's current state of affairs. She is acutely aware of Allan's inability to tolerate criticism; therefore, she labels herself as "selfish."

Understanding narcissistic vulnerability is central to working with this population. Interpretation is often experienced as criticism and should be avoided during the early stages of treatment. It is not uncommon for an individual to become offended by an ill-timed interpretation and use it to terminate treatment. Even when it appears that a positive therapeutic relationship has been established, an interpretation may be perceived negatively. For some individuals, however, interpretations are treated as interesting curiosities. Rather than producing emotional insights that lead to changes in behavior, they become the subject of intellectualized discussions or debates. Suffice it to say that interpretations should be used sparingly and judiciously with this population.

Protection of the fragile self is central to narcissistic pathology. Personal histories and family-of-origin dynamics are often described in ways that portray the person in a very favorable light. Even when the person's family life is depicted as being undesirable, the narcissistic individual will paint himself or herself as a heroic survivor. Sometimes, personal and family histories are vague and elusive. This was the case with Allan.

Relevant Personal History

Allan

Allan characterized his family life as "normal" and his parents as having been "loving." He said that his parents rarely argued and were permissive with him and his sister, who was 5 years his senior. He described her as quiet and aloof. He did not have much of a relationship with her. She left for college when he was 12 years old and did not return to the family home following graduation. Allan had few friends as a teenager. He spent most of his time studying and was not interested in sports or "fast cars." When he was a college junior, he dated a young woman for most of a year but ended that relationship when she "became too possessive." In graduate school he became seriously involved with another woman, but he ended that relationship when he discovered that she may have been dating other men "behind my back." He met Mary shortly after he relocated from California. It was a case of "love at first sight." He knew that she was "the one" and that he did not have to look any further.

Allan provided little additional information. As far as he was concerned, his marriage to Mary was a "happy one." They were going through a hard time but things would get better once his writing career got off the ground.

Assessment Findings

This couple's response to the written assessment process is illustrative of the spouses' nonverbalized (but not necessarily unconscious) agreement to protect each other and their marriage by not acknowledging any serious relationship difficulties. Their scores are reported below:

I. Dyadic Adjustment Scale

Mary	Allan
118	119

II. Images

Mary	Allan
D = 12%	D = 8%

III. Disaffection

Mary	Allan
30	28

IV. SIDCARB

	Mary	Allan
Factor I	64	62
Factor II	55	45
Factor III	50	50

V. Trust Scale

	Mary	Allan
Faith	65%	70%
Dependability	90%	95%
Predictability	87%	85%

VI. Intimacy Needs Questionnaire

	Mary	Allan
Total Intimacy Needs Strengths	525	495

Receptivity satisfaction and reciprocity satisfaction scores for all eight dimensions of intimacy were 100% for Allan. Only two dimensions of intimacy, emotional and psychological intimacy, were below 100% satisfaction for Mary. Both receptivity satisfaction and reciprocity satisfaction for these two subcomponents were 90%.

Feedback Session: Respecting the Couple's Defenses

A profile of this type usually means that the spouses are not yet ready to look critically at their relationship, for fear of what they might uncover. Their nonverbal request to the therapist is to "tread lightly." Feedback to the couple must be given in a way that reduces resistance and makes both spouses receptive to further clinical work. Aligning oneself with the couple's defenses can be a very effective way of gaining entry into the couple's system. This strategy is illustrated in the following excerpt.

Therapist: I'd like to begin today's session by reviewing the assessment findings with you. Would that be OK with you?

Mary: Yes.

Allan: Yes.

Therapist: Well, overall, there does not seem to be too much of a problem in your marriage—

Mary: Well, that is a relief to hear.

Allan: I told you that our problems were not very serious, just normal newlywed issues.

Mary: Yes, you were right.

Therapist: Let's take each instrument, one by one, and if you have any questions just ask me, OK?

Mary: OK.

Allan: Fine.

Therapist: The first instrument is the Dyadic Adjustment Scale. It was developed in 1976 and has been used to assess marital adjustment and satisfaction in thousands of studies. Validity was established by comparing the scores of divorced couples with scores of successfully married couples. Validity means that the test actually measures what it is intended to measure. The average score for satisfied couples was 114, for divorced couples it was 70. Mary, your score is 118. Allan, your score is 119. This means that both of you have adjusted well to married life and are very satisfied with each other.

Allan: That's good.

Mary: Yes, very good news.

Therapist: This next instrument was designed to assess how closely one's spouse matches his or her ideal partner. The scores are reported as difference scores or D-score percentages. The higher the D-score percentage, the more difference there is between one's actual partner and his or her ideal partner. The lower the D-score, the closer one's partner is to the ideal. The scale is called Images.

Mary, your D score is 12%. Allan, your D score is 8%. In my work with this measure over the last 25 years, I have found that D-score percentages that are more than 25% usually mean that there is considerable disappointment with one's partner. In my experience, scores of 12% and 8% are fairly normal. I think that even in the best of marriages there will be some discrepancy. In your case, both of you seem to have found the ideal partner. Let's take a look at your Images forms. (Hands measures to the couple).

Mary, the items where you see the greatest discrepancies are 5, 6, 7, and 8. These all fall into the same category or factor—empathy and understanding. Allan, you also identified discrepancies for the same items. This means that both of you are on the same page and that is good. Some work in empathic sharing and communication should help clear up these discrepancies to a large degree.

Mary: Dr. Bagarozzi, I think we really need some help in this area.

Allan: I agree. I don't think Mary really knows how important my writing is to me.

Mary: And I don't think Allan understands what having a family means to me.

Therapist: I think that these are excellent examples of where communication and empathy training can be very helpful.

Allan: I hope so.

Mary: So do I.

Therapist: This next scale is called the Disaffection Scale. Disaffection is defined as the gradual loss of emotional attachment, caring, positive feelings, and interest in one's partner. The higher the score, the more the Disaffection. Scores range from 21 to 84. Both of your scores are very low. Mary, your score is 30. Allan, your score is 28. These scores show that you really love and care about each other in more than just a romantic way. There is a real connection between the two of you. This connection is also evident in how both of you responded to the Intimacy Needs Questionnaire. (Hands the couple this questionnaire.)

This questionnaire breaks intimacy down into three parts. The first part, roman numerals I to VIII, measures the strength of each separate component need for intimacy. The strength for each component ranges from 1 to 100. Total intimacy needs strength scores range from 8 to 800. Average scores range between 450 and 650. Your total intimacy needs strength score, Mary, is 525. Allan, yours is 495. Both of these scores are in the average range.

Intimacy is a two-way street. In order for us to feel intimately connected, we must feel understood. Our partner must be experienced as being receptive to us and to what we have to share—that is, what we feel is important. This feeling of being heard and understood by our partner is called receptivity. That is the second score. The third score is the reciprocity score. In order to feely truly connected and intimate, we must get feedback from our partner in response to what we have shared. An intimate exchange is one where our partner shares his or her feelings about the issue or topic that concerns us. Do you have any questions about these three components of intimacy?

Mary: So just sharing your feelings is not enough?

Therapist: Correct. We need feedback. We need to know the other person's feelings in order to close the communication circuit. That's what makes the intimate connection. The give and take of communication.

Allan: But what if you don't agree with the other person's point of view?

Therapist: You can still be receptive and disagree. Receptivity does not mean agreement. It simply means understanding. Even if you disagree and say so, you are still being receptive, but you are also being reciprocal. You've let Mary know how you feel about something that is important to her, even if you disagree. For example, when it is time to have children.

For both receptivity satisfaction and reciprocity satisfaction, a percentage score is calculated. The higher the percentage scores for each of the eight areas of intimacy, the higher the satisfaction. Percentage scores below 70% are usually considered to be a cause for concern. Do you have any questions about the scoring process?

Mary: Can you go over the scoring again?

Therapist: Of course. There are three scores, Total needs strengths. This is the sum of all component needs strengths.

Mary: I got that.

Therapist: Receptivity is how much you feel understood and heard.

Mary: OK.

Therapist: Reciprocity is the feedback score.

Mary: OK.

Allan: And the percentage score is the satisfaction.

Therapist: That's right. The higher the percentage, the higher the satisfaction. Are there any more questions?

Allan: What do you think of our scores?

Therapist: Well, your scores for receptivity and reciprocity satisfaction are as close as you can get to perfect scores. There does not seem to be any problem in this area of your relationship. Shall we go to the next scale?

Allan: These tests scores are turning out to be pretty good.

Therapist: Yes, they are.

DISCUSSION

A standard practice in providing assessment feedback to a couple is to focus first on the strengths and positive aspects of the spouses' relationship before addressing those issues that require attention. This is particularly important for work with narcissistic individuals, who are highly sensitive to any criticism. Another tactic that is useful in avoiding perceived criticism is to depathologize the therapeutic process by stressing the educational and skills acquisition components of therapy. Referring to Images and pointing out that both Mary and Allan are in agreement that communication and empathy are of some concern allows the therapist to target Allan's empathic failure, a central issue in the treatment of narcissistic individuals, without singling him out.

It is important to keep in mind the narcissist's need for acceptance, approval, and praise. Allan's self-congratulatory comments about the assessment findings are an example of approval-seeking. The therapist's acknowledgment of these positive findings is an example of therapeutic mirroring. Therapeutic mirroring, during the early stages of treatment, is critical to the establishment of a positive therapeutic relationship. It reduces defensiveness and paves the way for the development of rudimentary empathy later in therapy (Bromberg, 1986).

SIDCARB and the Trust Scale were the final instruments to be discussed, since these were the measures where dissatisfactions were identified by Mary.

Therapist: These last two questionnaires are the ones that allow us to get a more precise picture of how external circumstances are affecting your marriage. I'd like to focus first on SIDCARB. Do you have any questions before we look at these last two questionnaires?

Allan: No.

Mary: No.

Therapist: Most couples who come for marriage counseling cite communication as a problem area in their relationship. You both have identified communication and empathy, which is a central aspect of functional communication, on SIDCARB and Images as areas of concern. Since functional communication is essential for a successful marriage, many instruments designed to assess marital satisfaction include questions about communication. Learning to communicate effectively, therefore, is an important part of the counseling process. If there is ample time remaining, we can begin communication skills training today after we discuss these two questionnaires.

Let's look at the first 10 questions of SIDCARB. These are the questions that pinpoint those areas of your relationship where you would like to see some changes in your partner's behavior. Allan, in addition to communication, you have identified in-laws and children as areas of concern. Mary, you have identified children and finances, so there is pretty much agreement about where the bulk of our work will be.

Now if you will review the Trust Scale with me, you will see that the only area of your marriage where there are some questions about trust is in the domain of faith in your partner. Mary, your percentage score is 65%. Allan, your percentage score is 70%.

Allan: When I look at my answers to the questions in the faith section, I see that I'm not so sure that Mary will always be as supportive of me and my work as she is now.

Therapist: Yes, I was going to ask you about your uncertainty—what you were thinking about when you answered questions 2 and 7 as you did.

Mary: You know I will be supportive of you and your work, Allan. I always have been and that will never change.

Allan: That's good to hear. I was unsure.

Therapist: Mary, your concern about Allan seems to be in the area of couple decision-making. Specifically questions 3, 4, and 6. What were your thoughts as you were answering those questions?

Mary: I was thinking of Allan leaving his job and not talking to me about it beforehand or sharing his feelings about his job with me or telling me about his plans about work before we got married. Now I know it was just a problem with the way we were communicating. I do trust you, Allan, and I do have faith that we will talk things over in the future before anyone makes a decision.

Therapist: This clears something up for me. I was going to ask you about question 15. You circled "strongly agree" with the statement: "I feel very uncomfortable when my partner has to make decisions that will affect me personally" in the predictability section of the Trust Scale.

Many of your difficulties stem from poor communication, as far as I can tell.

Mary: Yes, I feel a lot better about us now, and I know it will get better the more we learn to communicate.

DISCUSSION

How much information the therapist shares with the couple about the assessment measures depends upon a number of factors. Level of education, psychology mindedness, interest, attention span, and so on must be taken into account. The degree of defensiveness, personality dynamics, and the nature of the couple's relationship must also be considered in deciding what to discuss with the couple and how to discuss it. Collusive denial, rationalization, and externalization were the primary defenses used by Allan and Mary to avoid dealing with substantial relationship conflicts. By agreeing with Allan and Mary that the sources of their difficulties were "external," defensiveness was reduced to some degree. Attributing their problems to faulty communication made it possible for the couple to focus on their conflicts while still maintaining the myth of a happy and satisfying marriage.

The therapeutic technique of consolidation was used with this couple. Consolidation is helpful in reducing anxiety in a spouse who is likely to become defensive when his or her partner asks for changes that are perceived to be excessive, unrealistic, and challenging. With narcissistic individuals, there is always the possibility that requests for change will be experienced as attacks on the self (i.e., competence and worthiness), which may lead to the unilateral termination of treatment. To avoid such narcissistic wounding, the therapist consolidates, bundles, or groups several change requests under a single rubric so that they are perceived as being part of one manageable, slightly larger issue. In this couple's case, many of Mary's requests for change identified on SIDCARB and the Trust Scale were consolidated under the benign heading of a jointly agreed upon need for improved communication. This made it easier for the couple to "communicate better" about finances and children. The following exchanges illustrate this point.

Therapist: Good afternoon, folks. How are you today?
Allan: Good. I just sent one of my short stories out for review.
Therapist: That's exciting. I wish you all the best.
Allan: Thanks.
Therapist: Did you find some time to practice the communication skills we worked on last session?
Mary: Yes, we did. We practiced twice as you had suggested.
Therapist: How did your practice go?
Mary: Very well. We did what you told us to do. We only talked about the things that are good in our marriage. We also added talking about what we are thankful for and that was uplifting.
Therapist: Sounds like you are making progress.
Allan: I think we are.
Therapist: Today, I'd like you to use those communication skills to discuss some of the issues you identified on SIDCARB, if that is OK with you.
Mary: That's all right.
Allan: That's fine.
Therapist: I'd like to start with your concerns about in-laws, Allan. Is that OK with you?
Allan: Yes.
Therapist: Now, I'd like you to get into your talking and listening modes to discuss this issue. I'll get into my teaching and coaching role and help you out if you need some help. Allan, why don't you begin. Mary, you summarize.
Allan: Mary, I feel uncomfortable when I am around your family. I feel that they are watching me and thinking that I am avoiding getting a job. I think that they are judging me.
Mary: OK. You are uncomfortable around my family. You think that they are judging you because you don't have a job.
Allan: No, not exactly. I think they think I don't want to get a job. They don't consider my writing real work.
Mary: So you think that they believe you don't want to work and that your writing is not real work.
Allan: Yes.
Mary: But, that's not true. They are just concerned about our happiness, that's all.
Therapist: You both are doing fine. Mary, can you try to put yourself in Allan's place and try to feel like what it must be like to be him right now?
Mary: OK.
Therapist: Tell Allan what you think it must be like for him.
Mary: Allan, I think you feel misunderstood and a little angry with my parents for not being supportive of your work. Is that right?
Allan: Very much so.
Therapist: Is there anything else, Mary, that you think Allan might be feeling or thinking about this situation?

Mary: I don't know. Maybe you think that they don't like you. Maybe you think that they think I made a mistake when I married you.

Allan: That thought has crossed my mind.

Mary: But that's not true. They are just concerned about our welfare, that's all. They never have said a bad thing about you and that's the truth.

Therapist: Mary, it sounds like you have a good sense of how Allan feels and how he sees this situation. Allan, what do you think?

Allan: Yes, she does, but I'm still not sure about her parents' true feelings.

Mary: Well, I am. I've known them all my life.

Allan: OK.

Therapist: Allan, now it's your turn to put yourself in Mary's shoes. How do you think she feels about this situation?

Allan: I don't know. I really don't know how she sees things or how she feels.

Therapist: Try to put yourself in her place.

Allan: I don't know. Maybe angry.

Mary: No, I am not angry, Allan. I am—

Therapist: Mary, let Allan try to put himself in your place. Allan, go on, you are doing fine.

Allan: I'm really not sure.

Therapist: Let's pretend that Mary is a character in one of your short stories. You know the plot. How might she feel? How might she see you?

Allan: Maybe sad and frightened about her future.

Mary: Yes, I'm not angry. I'm scared.

Therapist: Allan, that was right on target about Mary's feelings. How might the woman in your short story see you? What might she think about you in this situation?

Allan: I don't know. In the handout you gave us about communication, it says not to "mind read." This sounds like you are asking me to read Mary's mind.

Therapist: That's a good point, but there is a difference. When someone "mind reads," he is usually convinced that he knows what the other person is thinking and then acts as if his convictions were, in fact, true. He doesn't communicate his convictions and doesn't ask for feedback. He just believes he knows what the other person is thinking. What I am asking you both to do is to try to see things from the other's perspective and then to check out and verify your accuracy. You are correct, Allan, it would be "mind reading" if you did not ask for feedback from Mary.

Now, how might the woman in your short story see her husband?

Allan: Maybe she would see him as fearful also. She sees his struggle and loves him.

Therapist: Mary, what are your thoughts? Give Allan some feedback.

Mary: Allan, I don't think you are afraid, but I do see you as struggling and, of course, I do love you very much.

Allan: That feels good to know.

Therapist: You both have done very well with this role reversal exercise. Some people have a hard time getting the knack of it, but you got it pretty quickly.

Allan: Thanks.

Therapist: You both deserve praise. I'd like you to incorporate role reversal when you practice your communication skills at home.

Mary: We can do that.

Allan: No problem.

DISCUSSION

Positive reinforcement and praise are used routinely throughout the therapeutic process and are considered to be essential components of behavioral exchange approaches to marital therapy. For some narcissistic individuals, there is always the possibility that positive reinforcement will be interpreted as admiration, which would feed the grandiose self. For others, however, praise may be interpreted as envy, which could lead to devaluation of the therapist and termination of treatment. The potential for such interpretations is reduced, to some degree, by stressing the accomplishments made by the couple as a unit.

Clearly, the focus of therapy with narcissistic individuals is the development of rudimentary empathy. The content of the couple's discussions is important, but fostering empathic understanding as much as possible is the primary objective. The less threatened the narcissistic spouse feels, the more he or she will be able to decenter and move from an egocentric and defensive position to a more relational one. It is unrealistic to expect that Allan will be able to relate to Mary as a separate individual in her own right, given the constraints of short-term problem-focused therapy, but the therapist can structure the couple's communication-interaction process in ways that make the development of empathy more likely by assigning role-taking exercises as an integral part of the couple's homework.

The therapist should also be aware that the acquisition of role-taking and empathic listening skills is much more difficult for narcissistic and borderline individuals than it is for most individuals seen in marital therapy, since projection, projective identification, idealization, merging, and magical thinking can interfere with the process. In the above example, when Allan is asked to put himself in "Mary's shoes," he projects his anger onto her. It is at such times that the therapist's structure and guidance are critical. Each time the narcissistic spouse is asked to reverse perspective, the therapist must make sure that his or her comments accurately reflect the partner's feelings and perspectives.

Another tactic that one can employ to help a spouse decenter is to encourage the use of the observing component of the person's ego. Typically, this ego function is poorly developed in narcissistic individuals. In the above example, Allan is asked to step outside himself and to picture himself through the eyes of a fictional character of his own creation. Doing so allows him to get some emotional distance from the issue at hand, reduces anxiety to some degree, and strengthens his capacity for self-observation, which is an important treatment goal with this population.

Several weeks into the therapy, when Allan and Mary came in for their appointment. Allan was visibly depressed and Mary was tense.

Therapist: Good evening. Nice to see you.
Mary: Doctor, Allan just got some bad news. His latest short story was rejected.
Therapist: Allan, I am very sorry. I know that you were very hopeful about this particular piece of work.
Allan: Yes. It is a big disappointment. I still think it is a good story, but the editor at the *New Yorker* didn't think so.
Therapist: I suspect their rejection rate is pretty high.
Allan: It is.
Therapist: And the competition is pretty stiff.
Allan: That's for sure.
Therapist: I remember what you said at our first meeting. Many famous writers' works were rejected initially, but that didn't stop them.
Allan: I know, but I thought this one was a good one.
Mary: Doctor, I've told Allan there are other magazines that he could submit his work to—magazines with a higher acceptance rate.
Therapist: How do you feel about Mary's suggestion?
Allan: She's right. I can try some others.
Mary: But, that's not the only problem. We have had some unexpected expenses, and we really need to do something about our finances. We are lucky that our insurance covers our therapy, so that's not a problem for us, but we have some big expenses coming up.
Therapist: I understand. Financial pressures are stressful for a couple. Allan, what are your thoughts about your financial situation?
Allan: Mary is right. It is not good.
Therapist: What are your options?
Mary: One of my father's friends owns a chain of newspapers and he has a position open as an editorial assistant. I wish Allan would consider it.
Therapist: Allan, what are your thoughts about this possibility?
Allan: I'm not an editor. I am a writer.
Mary: But you would make an excellent editor, and it would help us out in the meantime.
Allan: That's flunky work. It's not even writing a column.
Mary: But it is a start. Maybe they'll let you do a column once you have been there for a while.
Therapist: What other options do the two of you have?
Mary: I probably can get a raise from my father, but I really don't want him to know how bad this situation is, and I'm sure it would reflect badly on Allan if I did.
Allan: I agree we can't ask your father for any help. He'll really think I'm a deadbeat, for sure.
Mary: Doctor, do you have any suggestions?
Therapist: Have you looked at all your options?
Mary: I think we have. What do you think is the best one?

Therapist: I don't know what is best for you. Only you and Allan can make that decision. I know how difficult this must be for both of you. You have talked about three options. Let's review them together.
Mary: OK.
Therapist: The first is to continue along the path you are on now. The second would be for Allan to apply for an editorial position. The third would be to ask your father for financial help in the form of a raise. Am I correct?
Mary: Yes, but I guess we could use our credit cards for a while. I really don't want to do that.
Allan: Neither do I.
Therapist: So that is not an option.
Mary: Correct.
Mary: Allan, you know I have faith in you, but would you please consider looking into the editorial position? You still would have time to do your writing, I'm sure.
Allan: I guess I'll have to consider it. There does not seem to be much of a choice.
Therapist: Allan, I think I know how hard this decision must be for you. I know how much your independence means to you. I wonder if by applying for this editorial job you think that you will be seen as dependent on someone else?
Allan: A little.
Mary: Doctor, I've said to Allan that this is only a stepping stone.
Allan: (To Mary.) You think I'm too proud.
Mary: No, but maybe just a little stubborn.
Allan: Maybe just a little.
Therapist: Sometimes, we have to put our personal needs and desires on a back burner for a while for the sake of our relationship.
Mary: Sometimes, we have to sacrifice. Isn't that the way it is in marriage, Doctor?
Therapist: I tend to think of it as a noble thing to do for one's spouse and family.

DISCUSSION

The rejection of another short story made it difficult for Allan to continue denying his feelings of disappointment and dejection. Mary is supportive, but she is also concerned and pragmatic. The realities of the couple's financial circumstances cannot be ignored any longer. It is not uncommon in relationships where one of the partners is narcissistic for his or her spouse to serve as a reality check, since reality testing is often hampered by the narcissistic spouse's grandiosity. Even though Mary has learned to do this in a way that does not exacerbate the narcissistic wound that Allan has suffered, he still becomes defensive. The therapist steps in to deescalate the conflict by having the couple approach the problem as one that is external to their relationship rather than one that exists between the two partners. This echoes the couple's initial presentation of their difficulties as being "circumstantial."

The potential for the therapist to become triangulated surfaces when Mary asks him to recommend a solution. This is avoided by referring the issue back to the couple for consideration. Suggesting a solution also would play into the narcissistic fantasy of an omnipotent and omniscient idealized person who will take care of the couple's needs. Later, the therapist can be blamed and devalued if the suggested solution proves to be inadequate.

One of the greatest fears of the narcissist is dependency. To be dependent upon another engenders envy and leaves the person vulnerable and open to exploitation. Addressing this issue with Allan must be done tactfully and in a way that models empathy. Sensitivity to criticism and perceived slights can trigger a paranoid reaction in some individuals. Asking Allan to apply for a position that he believes to be beneath him has been experienced, in the past, as a negative comment about his competence. One way to make such a suggestion more palatable is to present it in a way that makes it possible for him to rationalize his acceptance as a magnanimous gesture of altruism. The therapist does not endorse Mary's characterization of Allan's consideration of her suggestion as sacrificial, however, in order to avoid the possibility of Allan taking on a martyr role in the marriage.

Allan was able to secure a position as an editorial assistant, and this made the couple's relationship less stressful. The couple was asked to complete only two assessment measures at the conclusion of treatment: SIDCARB and the Trust Scale, since these were the only two instruments in which Mary had voiced moderate concerns. Mary's factor I score on SIDCARB was 56, Allan's was 55. Scores on the faith dimension of the Trust Scale were 85% for Mary and 89% for Allan. Dependability and predictability scores for both spouses also increased by a few percentage points. Based upon these post-treatment findings, therapy was successful in that the spouses were satisfied with the outcome. From an outsider's perspective, the gains were modest. For Mary and Allan, however, they were significant. The couple was no longer in crisis; Allan had a steady job; Mary's parents were more positively disposed toward Allan; communication, problem solving, and conflict negotiation between the spouses had improved; and Allan's empathy and role-taking skills were a little better than they had been before the couple entered treatment. Even though the narcissist's capacity for empathy is severely limited, he or she may have an uncanny ability to "read" people and feign empathy in order to manipulate them. Allan's perceived progress in this area in such a short time must be considered in this light.

Abrupt termination of treatment is always a possibility with narcissistic individuals, who tend to remain in therapy only as long as they find it personally useful and ego-gratifying, and as long as it does not threaten their fragile self-esteem. One can never know what will produce a narcissistic wound that triggers a negative therapeutic reaction. Therefore, the therapist must decide if and when to deal with a couple's nonverbalized or unconscious mutually protective contractual agreements. In Allan and Mary's case, it was decided that doing so would be too threatening and countertherapeutic. Consequently, the couple's denial and externalization of their problems was not addressed.

Collusive contractual agreements are hierarchically ordered in terms of their conscious accessibility and degree of threat to the self. In short-term problem focused treatment, only those contracts that the therapist believes can be dealt with successfully in this brief format should be explored. Here again, this is a judgment call for the therapist.

STUDY QUESTIONS

1. In Appendix C, guidelines designed to help borderline and narcissistic individuals communicate more effectively are presented. Can you think of any additional guidelines that you believe would be helpful in working with this population? If so, describe them below and explain your reasons for including them.
2. When Paul and Tina failed to complete their sensate focus homework, the therapist took responsibility for the couple's failure by suggesting that the assignment might have been ill timed and premature. This was followed by a restraining technique, which proved to be effective in helping the couple resume sexual relations to a limited degree. What are some other strategies that the therapist might have used to achieve this end?
3. The joining strategy used with Allan and Mary is called "aligning with the couple's collusion." It is particularly helpful in reducing defensiveness with individuals who are extremely sensitive to criticism, making them more receptive to other direct forms of intervention as the therapeutic process unfolds. For example, Allan was receptive when he was urged to put himself in Mary's place and to "pretend" that she was a character in one of his short stories. This is only one example of training in role taking and empathy. Can you think of other techniques that might facilitate role taking and the development of rudimentary forms of empathy that could have been used with this couple?

Epilogue

Collusion between partners and spouses is a universal phenomenon. Collusive pacts, whether they are consciously agreed upon contracts or unconsciously negotiated arrangements, serve two basic functions: to protect the partners' respective selves and to preserve dyadic homeostasis. Couples enter treatment when these collusive agreements have failed in some way, resulting in a destabilization of the system. Most couples who seek professional assistance desire a return to their previously existing defensive status quo, which usually requires only minor changes in their formerly negotiated collusive agreements. If the spouses experience the therapist's attempts to help as asking them to make personal or systemic changes that they are unable or unwilling to make, the couple will mobilize their defenses to neutralize or defeat the therapist.

Collusions present in a variety of forms and guises. It is hoped that after reading this volume, therapists will be able to identify some of the lesser-known types more easily. Resistance to change is to be expected in therapy and should not be seen as an annoyance or distraction. Working through resistance is the crux of therapy. How one goes about this process is a matter of personal style and creativity. The brief problem-focused approach outlined in this text relies heavily upon the use of pretreatment assessment tools and procedures that, as far as the couple is concerned, are the focus of treatment. The couple's collusive defenses and contracts are dealt with subtly and in an understated fashion. The contractual agreement between the couple and the therapist is to resolve the presenting problems or conflicts and not to overhaul the couple's system. Therefore, only those collusive defenses and contracts that stand in the way of successful conflict resolution and problem-solving are targeted. For many couples, resolution of the presenting problem or conflict marks the end of their treatment. For other couples, however, there may be the realization that additional personal and/or dyadic work is needed before a successful and satisfying relationship can develop. In such cases, resolution of the presenting problem or conflict represents only the first leg of a longer therapeutic journey.

The collusive pacts made between partners when borderline or narcissistic pathology is part of the clinical picture are characterized by primitive defensive operations that exist for the protection of extremely fragile selves. Understanding the central differences between these two diagnostic entities is essential for conducting treatment and achieving realistic therapeutic outcomes. In my experience with such couples, I have found that it is not unusual for them to return for additional short-term therapy when new conflicts arise or when they are confronted by difficult developmental challenges. Maintaining contact with a therapist who is experienced as a constant, understanding, supportive person is important for these couples. Responding to a couple's brief note, greeting card, or letter long after formal treatment has been terminated may be all that is necessary to provide reassurance that there is a secure base to which they can return if the need arises.

Appendix A

FOLLOW-UP QUESTIONNAIRE

Marital/Couple Relationship

Please circle one response 1 = Very Little 10 = A Great Deal

1. If you sought help *with a partner* for a marital or relationship problem, to what degree do you think you learned to use the following skills by the end of treatment?
   (a) Functional communication 1 2 3 4 5 6 7 8 9 10
   (b) Problem solving 1 2 3 4 5 6 7 8 9 10
   (c) Conflict negotiation 1 2 3 4 5 6 7 8 9 10
   (d) Compromise 1 2 3 4 5 6 7 8 9 10
   (e) Empathy (understanding your partner's feelings) 1 2 3 4 5 6 7 8 9 10
   (f) Role taking (understanding how your partner perceives and experiences you) 1 2 3 4 5 6 7 8 9 10
2. To what extent do you and your partner use these same skills *today?*
   (a) Functional communication 1 2 3 4 5 6 7 8 9 10
   (b) Problem solving 1 2 3 4 5 6 7 8 9 10
   (c) Conflict negotiation 1 2 3 4 5 6 7 8 9 10
   (d) Compromise 1 2 3 4 5 6 7 8 9 10
   (e) Empathy (understanding your partner's feelings) 1 2 3 4 5 6 7 8 9 10
   (f) Role taking (understanding how your partner perceives and experiences you) 1 2 3 4 5 6 7 8 9 10

Please circle one response 1 = Not At All Satisfied
10 = Very Satisfied

3. By the end of treatment, how satisfied were you with your partner?

   1 2 3 4 5 6 7 8 9 10

4. How satisfied are you *today* with your partner?

   1 2 3 4 5 6 7 8 9 10

5. By the end of treatment, how satisfied were you with your marriage/ relationship?

   1 2 3 4 5 6 7 8 9 10

6. How satisfied are you *today* with your marriage/relationship?

   1 2 3 4 5 6 7 8 9 10

7. What aspects of therapy and the therapist's behavior do you believe to have been the least helpful? Please explain your answer and give suggestions for improvement below:
8. What aspects of therapy and the therapist's behavior do you believe to have been the most helpful? Please explain your answer below.

Appendix B

RELATIONSHIP PROBLEMS QUESTIONNAIRE

Part I

Please circle one response: 1 = Not At All Satisfied 10 = Very Satisfied

1. In general, how satisfied are you with your partner?

   1 2 3 4 5 6 7 8 9 10

2. In general, how satisfied are you with your relationship?

   1 2 3 4 5 6 7 8 9 10

3. In general, how satisfied are you with the intimacy you share with your partner?

   1 2 3 4 5 6 7 8 9 10

4. In general, how satisfied are you with how you and your partner communicate?

   1 2 3 4 5 6 7 8 9 10

5. In general, how satisfied are you with how you and your partner express your love and affection for each other?

   1 2 3 4 5 6 7 8 9 10

6. In general, how satisfied are you in your sexual relationship with your partner?

   1 2 3 4 5 6 7 8 9 10

7. In general, how satisfied are you with the financial aspects of your life with your partner?

   1 2 3 4 5 6 7 8 9 10

Please circle one response: 1 = Not At All Satisfied 10 = Very Satisfied

8. In general, how satisfied are you with the division of labor in your relationship and the role relationships that exist between you and your partner?

   1 2 3 4 5 6 7 8 9 10

9. In general, how satisfied are you with how your partner relates to your children and his or her relationship with them?

   1 2 3 4 5 6 7 8 9 10

10. In general, how satisfied are you with the way that your partner handles his or her household management responsibilities?

    1 2 3 4 5 6 7 8 9 10

11. In general, how satisfied are you with your relationship with your partner's parents, relatives, etc., and their effect upon you as a couple?

    1 2 3 4 5 6 7 8 9 10

12. In general, how satisfied are you with your partner's friends and your friends and their effect upon your relationship as a couple?

    1 2 3 4 5 6 7 8 9 10

13. In general, how satisfied are you with your partner's work, job, profession, and its impact upon your relationship?

    1 2 3 4 5 6 7 8 9 10

14. In general, how satisfied are you with your own work, job, profession, and its impact upon your relationship?

    1 2 3 4 5 6 7 8 9 10

Please circle one response: 1 = Not At All Satisfied 10 = Very Satisfied

15. In general, how satisfied are you with how you and your partner spend your leisure time together as a couple?

    1 2 3 4 5 6 7 8 9 10

16. In general, how satisfied are you with the religious/spiritual dimension of your life as a couple?

    1 2 3 4 5 6 7 8 9 10

17. In general, how satisfied are you with the way you and your partner deal with differences of opinion?

    1 2 3 4 5 6 7 8 9 10

18. In general, how satisfied are you with how you and your partner solve problems as a couple?

    1 2 3 4 5 6 7 8 9 10

19. In general, how satisfied are you with how you and your partner resolve conflicts as a couple?

    1 2 3 4 5 6 7 8 9 10

20. To what extent are you satisfied with the degree to which your partner meets your overall expectations for this relationship?

    1 2 3 4 5 6 7 8 9 10

Part II

If any of the following issues constitute a current source of conflict in your relationship, rate the degree of severity of the conflict for all that apply.

Please circle one response: 1 = Not At All Severe 10 = Very Severe

1. Power struggles 1 2 3 4 5 6 7 8 9 10
2. Conflicts over values 1 2 3 4 5 6 7 8 9 10
3. Relationships with friends 1 2 3 4 5 6 7 8 9 10

4. Relationships with family members 1 2 3 4 5 6 7 8 9 10
5. Emotional or sexual involvements 1 2 3 4 5 6 7 8 9 10
6. Partner's personal problems 1 2 3 4 5 6 7 8 9 10
7. My personal problems 1 2 3 4 5 6 7 8 9 10
8. Conflicts over conventionality 1 2 3 4 5 6 7 8 9 10
9. Conflicts over intimacy 1 2 3 4 5 6 7 8 9 10
10. Partner's jealousy 1 2 3 4 5 6 7 8 9 10
11. My jealousy 1 2 3 4 5 6 7 8 9 10
12. Problems with previous spouses or relationships 1 2 3 4 5 6 7 8 9 10

Please circle one response: 1 = Not At All Severe 10 = Very Severe

13. Problems with stepchildren 1 2 3 4 5 6 7 8 9 10
14. Personal illnesses 1 2 3 4 5 6 7 8 9 10
15. Partner's illnesses 1 2 3 4 5 6 7 8 9 10
16. Personal physical handicaps 1 2 3 4 5 6 7 8 9 10
17. Partner's physical handicaps 1 2 3 4 5 6 7 8 9 10
18. Partner's alcoholism or addiction 1 2 3 4 5 6 7 8 9 10
19. Your own alcoholism or addiction 1 2 3 4 5 6 7 8 9 10
20. Verbal abuse from partner 1 2 3 4 5 6 7 8 9 10
21. Physical abuse from partner 1 2 3 4 5 6 7 8 9 10
22. Sexual abuse from partner 1 2 3 4 5 6 7 8 9 10
23. Psychological abuse from partner 1 2 3 4 5 6 7 8 9 10
24. Partner as survivor of physical, sexual abuse, or incest 1 2 3 4 5 6 7 8 9 10
25. Self as survivor of physical, sexual abuse, or incest 1 2 3 4 5 6 7 8 9 10
26. Other issues not listed 1 2 3 4 5 6 7 8 9 10

    Explain ____

Not At All Very

27. How committed are you to your partner? 1 2 3 4 5 6 7 8 9 10
28. How committed are you to the relationship? 1 2 3 4 5 6 7 8 9 10
29. How willing are you to make changes in your personal behavior in order to improve your relationship? 1 2 3 4 5 6 7 8 9 10
30. How willing would you be to separate from your partner if he or she does not change his or her behavior in order to improve your relationship? 1 2 3 4 5 6 7 8 9 10

Appendix C

GUIDELINES FOR SPEAKERS AND RECEIVERS

SPEAKER'S GUIDELINES

1. When it is your turn to speak, speak in short, concise sentences so that your partner will be able to repeat, word for word, what you have said. By repeating what you have said accurately, you will know that your partner has understood your message. Before you speak, think carefully about what you want to say. Gather your thoughts and speak slowly. When you have finished, ask your partner to repeat what you have said. If your partner repeats what you have said accurately, tell him or her so and then go on to your next thought. Once you both have mastered the "word for word" repetition, you can move on to summarizing. This will speed up the process considerably.

Comments

The emphasis upon speaking slowly and deliberately and thinking clearly about what one wants to communicate before making any statement targets impulse-control problems. It also helps the speaker to focus his or her attention on one issue at a time. This is very helpful for individuals whose thinking is scattered, circumstantial, or tangential. The therapist's responsibility is to help the person remain focused and not to ramble or become distracted. The therapist also models patience and calmness while teaching these skills.

2. When you speak, separate your thoughts from your feelings. Don't confuse what you think about your partner with how you feel about him or her. Take full responsibility for what you think and for how you feel. For example, say "I feel sad, angry, happy," and so on, rather than "you make me sad, angry, happy," or "I think you are not being honest" and not "I feel you are not being honest."

Comments

For many people who function at this level of personality organization, emotions often cloud their thinking, judgment, and behavior. When thoughts are different from feelings, confusion is less likely to occur, and the person will be more likely to think before giving vent to his or her emotions or acting upon them.

Having the person take full responsibility for his or her feelings and thoughts deals directly with externalization, projection, and projective identification. This can limit their use, to some degree, while the couple is in the therapist's presence, but it will not correct the underlying dynamics and structural problems associated with splitting. For such changes to be effected, long-term individual treatment is necessary. Nevertheless, couples who are able to learn these skills are usually more successful at conflict negotiation than those who cannot.

3. Do not try to read your partner's mind or attribute negative motives or intentions to him or her. If you are uncertain about your partner's intentions, don't accuse him or her; ask for an explanation. Once you have received such an explanation, you can tell your partner how you perceived the behavior and interpreted his or her motives. Keep in mind that these are your own interpretations and perceptions, and they may not be accurate. Take your partner's explanations at "face value."

Comments

This guideline is designed to deal with the suspiciousness and sensitivity to perceived slights to which borderline and narcissistic individuals are particularly vulnerable. Criticism of any type, whether justified or not, is experienced as a deep wounding. Depression and rage are common reactions. It is not uncommon for a spouse to abruptly terminate treatment immediately after having been criticized by his or her partner or after receiving an untimely interpretation from the therapist that is perceived as a criticism and/or attack. Simple observations and comments by the therapist about a couple's interaction style may also be perceived as an attack upon the couple's defense system, and couples may collusively use this as a reason for discontinuing therapy. Here again, it would be erroneous to think that this simple exercise would be sufficient to alter longstanding perceptual patterns, cognitive structures, and belief systems, but there are some benefits.

First, since both spouses are asked to adhere to the same guidelines, neither partner feels that he or she is being singled out as having a problem in this area.

Second, the implied assumption is that neither spouse is bad or malintentioned; this facilitates collaboration between the partners and the therapist.

Third, the couple will think of the therapist as one who sees both spouses in a positive light, thus strengthening the therapist's role as a neutral facilitator and teacher.

4. Say exactly what you mean, think, and feel. Do not send hidden messages or messages with implied meanings. Don't expect your partner to "read your mind." Be direct, but be polite and diplomatic.

Comments

When ego boundaries are porous and tenuous, mind reading is often expected. A mild form of this often appears in the early stages of some romantic relationships, when lovers expect their partners to know what they need, want, and desire without having to ask for it. Eventually, this romantic fantasy is replaced by more mature and realistic expectations as the relationship develops. However, this fantasy is never completely given up, since its roots lie in the early infant-mother symbiosis that did once exist.

For individuals who function at a borderline level of personality organization, the expectation of mind reading is symptomatic of good self/good object, bad self/bad object fusion and an incomplete process of separation-individuation. There is no need for verbal communication when self and object are joined in this primitive fashion. Reading one's spouse's mind actually represents the belief in one's own projections. A therapist can easily become the focal point of a spouse or couple's mind-reading belief and expectations.

As stated earlier, it would be incorrect to assume that such simple exercises in functional communication can significantly change the spouses' beliefs about mind reading. However, mind reading can be reduced and managed to some degree when these skills are used under a therapist's supervision.

5. Do not use aggressive forms of communication. Aggressive communications do not lead to successful conflict negotiation and problem solving. They only lead to defensiveness, counterattack, and withdrawal. Some of the most common types of aggressive communications are attacking, threatening, blaming, criticizing, ridiculing, interrupting, and using sarcasm.

Comments

High levels of aggression coupled with weak ego boundaries, which are typical for such conditions, make this last speaker's guideline critical, since reducing negative reciprocity and increasing positive exchanges between partners is essential to therapeutic success.

RECEIVER'S GUIDELINES

1. Listen attentively to your partner and do not interrupt your partner while he or she is speaking. If for any reason you are unclear or have not understood what your partner has said, ask your partner for clarification or ask him or her to repeat the message.

Comments

This guideline is meant to help the person increase his or her ability to delay immediate gratification and to strengthen frustration tolerance. The maintenance and generalization of these ego skills, once therapy is terminated, depends upon the degree to which the spouses were successful in completing homework assignments designed for the practice of these skills. Typically couples are encouraged to practice these functional communication skills twice each week for a minimum of 40 minutes per practice session during the initial stages of treatment. As therapy progresses and couples begin to incorporate these skills into their everyday lives, practice sessions can be reduced to once a week. This guideline also helps with impulse control by requiring the listener to "wait" for his or her turn before speaking.

2. Accept whatever your partner says at "face value." Take everything that is said literally. Do not attribute hidden meanings to what is said and don't interpret what your partner says to you. If your partner says something that you believe to be factually incorrect, don't interrupt him or her. When it is your turn to speak, this issue can be addressed.

Comments

This guideline is complementary to speaker guideline 4, which deals with mind reading and suspiciousness. When there is a dispute about a factual matter, the therapist's role is to help the couple clarify the issue of concern. The partner who disputes the matter is asked to describe the incident as he or she remembers it. Next, that partner is asked to share his or her feelings, perceptions, and interpretations of the events in question.

Once this is done, the therapist does not attempt to uncover the "truth." Instead, the incident is positively connoted and treated as an example of two people simply remembering, perceiving, and interpreting the same event differently. The therapist further normalizes the experience by saying that it is a common occurrence in the lives of most couples. The therapist adds that by using their newly acquired communication skills, such "misunderstandings" are less likely to happen in the future. The success of this strategy depends to a great extent upon the degree to which paranoid thinking and suspiciousness are present. Nevertheless, it offers the couple a more positive alternative.

3. Try to put yourself in your partner's place, to see things through his or her eyes, and to experience yourself as your partner might experience you. Don't attribute your own thoughts, feelings, beliefs, and so on, to your partner. Imagine what it must be like to *be* your partner.

Comments

Although empathy and role taking are extremely difficult for most people with borderline and narcissistic conditions to experience, this does not mean that these skills should not be taught or that their behavioral components cannot be learned to some degree. This is an important aspect of having a spouse repeat his or her partner's statements word for word. Although the partner may be unable to experience what his or her mate experiences or to reverse perspectives, he or she is still required to hear them and acknowledge them openly.

4. When your partner is finished speaking, repeat back to him or her, word for word, what you have heard and understood.

Comments

This guideline addresses not only empathy and role taking but also validation of the speaker's self. The safety of the therapeutic setting and the positive structure of the communication guidelines make it possible for spouses to say what they think and feel, knowing that they will be heard, possibly for the first time. Guideline 5 provides an additional safety net for the speaker.

5. Listen carefully to what your partner has to say. Don't pass judgment on your partner's thoughts, beliefs, feelings, or viewpoints, even if you don't agree with them. Try to respect your differences.

Comments

Splitting contributes to dichotomous thinking. People are seen as either good or bad, viewpoints are seen as either right or wrong, and there are no shades of gray. Since structural change in the self cannot be expected, given the short-term format of therapy, the best that one can hope for is that differences can begin to be seen as merely differences and not in terms of polar opposites. The therapist can help bring about this change by encouraging spouses to generate a number of possible solutions to their problems and then help them consider both the positive and the negative aspects of each. By stressing the advantages of seeing a problem and its solution from different perspectives and not discussing the proposed options in terms of "rightness" or "wrongness," the therapist may be able to effect some cognitive modifications.

References

Adams, J. S. (1963). Toward an understanding of inequity. *Journal of Abnormal and Social Psychology, 67,* 422–436.

Adams, J. S. (1965). Inequity in social exchange. In L. Berkowitz (Ed.), *Advances in experimental social psychology* (Vol. 2). New York: Academic Press.

Althof, S. E. (2007). Treatment of rapid ejaculation: Psychotherapy, pharmacotherapy, and combined therapy. In S. R. Leiblum (Ed.), *Principles and practice of sex therapy* (pp. 212–240). New York: Guilford Press.

Anderson, S. A., & Bagarozzi, D. A. (1983). The use of family myths as an aid to strategic therapy. *Journal of Family Therapy, 5,* 145–154.

Anderson, S. A., & Bagarozzi, D. A. (1988). *Family myths: Psychotherapy implications.* New York: Haworth Press.

Anderson, S. A., Bagrozzi, D. A., & Giddings, C. W. (1986). Images: Preliminary scale construction. *American Journal of Family Therapy, 14,* 357–363.

Bagarozzi, D. A. (1981). The symbolic meaning of behavioral exchanges in marital therapy. In A. S. Gurman (Ed.), *Questions and answers in the practice of family therapy* (pp. 173–177). New York: Brunner/Mazel.

Bagarozzi, D. A. (1983). Methodological developments in measuring social exchange perspectives in marital dyads (SIDCARB): A new tool for clinical intervention. In D. A. Bagarozzi, A. P. Jurich, & A. W. Jackson (Eds), *Marital and family therapy: New perspectives in theory, research and practice* (pp. 79–104). New York: Human Sciences Press.

Bagarozzi, D. A. (1990). *Intimacy needs questionnaire.* Atlanta: Human Resources Consultants, unpublished instrument.

Bagarozzi, D. A. (2001). *Enhancing intimacy in marriage: A clinician's guide.* New York: Taylor & Francis.

Bagarozzi, D. A. (2008). Understanding and treating marital infidelity: A multidimensional model. *American Journal of Family Therapy, 36,* 1–17.

Bagarozzi, D. A. (2011). A closer look at couple collusion: Protecting the self and preserving the system. *American Journal of Family Therapy, 39,* 390–403.

Bagarozzi, D. A., & Anderson, S. A. (1982). The evolution of family mythological systems: Considerations for meaning, clinical assessment, and treatment. *Journal of Psychoanalytic Anthropology, 5,* 71–90.

Bagarozzi, D. A., & Anderson, S. A. (1988). Personal, conjugal and family myths: Theoretical, empirical and clinical developments. *Journal of Psychotherapy and the Family, 4*, 167–194.

Bagarozzi, D. A., & Anderson, S. A. (1989). *Personal, marital, and family myths: Theoretical formulations and clinical strategies*. New York: W. W. Norton.

Bagarozzi, D. A., & Atilano, R. B. (1982). SIDCARB: A clinical tool for rapid assessment of social exchange inequities and relationship barriers. *Journal of Sex and Marital Therapy, 8*, 325–334.

Bagarozzi, D. A., Bagarozzi, J. I. (1982). A theoretically derived model of premarital intervention: The making of a family system, *Clinical Social Work Journal, 10*, 52–62.

Bagarozzi, D. A., Bagarozzi, J. I., Anderson, S. A., & Pollane, L. (1984). Premarital education and training sequence (PETS): A three year follow-up of an experimental study. *Journal of Counseling and Development, 63*, 91–100.

Bagarozzi, D. A., & Pollane, L. (1983). A replication and validation of the Spousal Inventory of Desired Changes and Relationship Barriers (SIDCARB): Elaboration on diagnostic and clinical utilization. *Journal of Sex and Marital Therapy, 9*, 303–315.

Bagarozzi, D. A., & Wodarski, J. S. (1977). A social exchange typology of conjugal relationships and conflict development. *Journal of Marriage and Family Counseling, 3*, 53–60.

Bateson, G. (1935). Culture contact and schismogenesis. *Man, 35*, 148–183.

Bateson, G., Jackson, D. D., Haley, J., & Weakland, J. H. (1956). Toward a theory of schizophrenia. *Behavioral Science, 1*(1), 251–264.

Blood, R. O., & Wolfe, D. M. (1960). *Husbands and wives*. New York: the Free Press.

Boszormenyi-Nagy, I., & Spark, G. M. (1973). *Invisible loyalties: Reciprocity in intergenerational family therapy*. New York: Harper & Row.

Bray, J., Williamson, D., & Malone, E. (1984). Personal authority in the family system: Development of a questionnaire to measure personal authority in intergenerational family processes. *Journal of Marital and Family Therapy, 10*, 167–178.

Bromberg, P.M. (1986). The mirror and the mask: On narcissism and psychoanalytic growth. In A. P. Morrison (Ed.), *Essential papers on narcissism* (pp. 438–466). New York: New York University Press.

Busby, D. M., Christensen, C., Crane, D. R., & Larson, J. H. (1995). A revision of the Dyadic Adjustment Scale for use with distressed and non-distressed couples: Construct hierarchy and multidimensional scales. *Journal of Marital and Family Therapy, 21*, 2889–308.

Crane, D. R., Middleton, K. C., & Bean, R. A. (2000). Establishing criterion scores for the Kansas Marital Satisfaction Scale and the Revised Dyadic Adjustment Scale. *American Journal of Family Therapy*, 2, 53–60.

Dicks, H. (1967). *Marital tensions: Clinical studies toward a psychological theory of interaction*. London: Routledge and Kegan Paul.

Edwards, J. M. (1969). Familial behavior as social exchange. *Journal of Marriage and the Family, 31*, 518–527.

Erikson, E. (1963). *Childhood and society*. New York: W. W. Norton.

Erikson, E. (1968). *Identity youth and crisis*. New York: W. W. Norton.

Erikson, E. (1982). *The life cycle completed*. New York: W. W. Norton.

Fenichel, O. (1945). *The psychoanalytic theory of neuroses*. New York: W. W. Norton.

Ferreira, A. (1963). Family myths and homeostasis. *Archives of General Psychiatry, 9*, 457–463.

Giffin, M. E., Johnson, A.M., & Litin, E. M. (1954). The transmission of superego defects in the family. *American Journal of Orthopsychiatry, 24*, 668–684.

Gottman, J. (1994). *What predicts divorce?* Hillsdale, NJ: Erlbaum.

Haley, J. (1963). *Strategies of psychotherapy.* New York: Grune & Straton.

Homans, G. (1974). *Social behavior: Its elementary forms.* New York: Harcourt, Brace & World.

Johnson, A. M., & Szurek, S. A. (1952). The genesis of antisocial acting out in children and adults. *Psychoanalytic Quarterly, 21,* 323–343.

Kaplan, H. (1979). *Disorders of sexual desire and other new concepts and techniques in sex therapy.* New York: Brunner/Mazel.

Kayser, K. (1996). The Marital Disaffection Scale: An inventory for assessing emotional estrangement in marriage. *American Journal of Family Therapy, 24,* 83–88.

Kernberg, O. (1985). *Borderline conditions and pathological narcissism.* Northvale, NJ: Jason Aronson.

Lang, R. D. (1965). Mystification, confusion and conflict. In I. Boszormenyi-Nagy & J. L. Framo (Eds.), *Intensive family therapy. Theoretical and practical aspects* (pp. 343–363). New York: Harper & Row.

Lederer, W. J., & Jackson, D. D. (1956). *The mirages of marriage.* New York: W. W. Norton.

Levine, S. (1988). *Sex is not simple.* Columbus: Ohio Psychology.

Levinger, G. (1976). Social psychological perspectives on marital dissolution. *Journal of Social Issues, 32,* 21–47.

Lewis, R. A., & Spanier, G. B. (1979). Theorizing about the quality and stability of marriage. In W. R. Burr, R. Hill, F. Nye, & I. L. Reiss (Eds.), *Contemporary theories about the family* (Vol. 1). London: Free Press.

Locke, H. J., & Wallace, K. M. (1959). Short marital adjustment and predictions test: Their reliability and validity. *Marriage and Family Living, 21,* 251–255.

Mahler, M. (1968). *On human symbiosis and the vicissitudes of individuation: Vol. 1. Infantile psychosis.* New York: International Universities Press.

Masters, W., & Johnson, V. (1970). *Human sexual inadequacy.* Boston: Little Brown.

Masters, W. H., Johnson, V. E., & Kolodny, R. C. (1994). *Heterosexuality.* New York: Harper Collins.

Mruk, C. (1995). *Self-Esteem: Research, theory, and practice.* New York: Springer.

O'Brien, E., & Epstein, S. (1988). *MSEI: The multidimensional self-esteem inventory.* Odessa, FL: Psychological Assessment Resources.

Piper, W. E., & Joyce, A. (2001). Psychosocial treatment outcome. In W. J. Livesley (Ed.), *Handbook of personality disorder: Theory, research, and treatment* (pp. 323–343). New York: Guilford Press.

Rempel, J. K., Holmes, J. G., & Zanna, M. P. (1985). Trust in close relationships. *Journal of Personality and Social Psychology, 49,* 95–112.

Sager, C. (1976). *Marriage contracts and couple therapy: Hidden forces in intimate relationships.* New York: Brunner/Mazel.

Schumm, W. R., Jurich, A. P., & Bollman, S. R. (1981). The validity of Edmonds' Marital Conventionalization Scale. *Journal of Psychology, 109,* 65–71.

Snyder, D. K., & Regts, J. M. (1982). Factor scales for assessing marital disharmony and disaffection. *Journal of Consulting and Clinical Psychology, 50,* 736–743.

Spanier, G. (1976). Measuring dyadic adjustment: New scales for assessing the quality of marriage and similar dyads. *Journal of Marriage and the Family, 38,* 15–30.

Spanier, G. B., & Thompson, L. (1982). A confirmatory analysis of the Dyadic Adjustment Scale. *Journal of Marriage and the Family, 44,* 731–738.

Spector, I. P., Carey, M. P., & Steinberg, L. (1996). The Sexual Desire Inventory: Development, factor structure and evidence of reliability. *Journal of Sex and Marital Therapy, 22,* 175–190.

Sullivan, H. S. (1953). *The interpersonal theory of psychiatry.* New York: W. W. Norton.

Thibaut, J., & Kelly, H. H. (1959). *The social psychology of groups.* New York: Wiley.

Touliatos, J., Perlmutter, B. F., & Holden, G. W. (2001). *Handbook of family measurement techniques* (Vols. 1 & 2). Thousand Oaks, CA: Sage.

Touliatos, J., Perlmutter, B. F., & Straus, M. A. (2001). *Handbook of family measurement techniques* (Vol. 3). Thousand Oaks, CA: Sage.

Vogel, E. F., & Bell, N. W. (1960). The emotionally disturbed child as the family scapegoat. In N. W. Bell & E. F. Vogel (Eds.), *A modern introduction to the family* (pp. 382–397). Glencoe, IL. The Free Press.

Waller, W., & Hill, R. (1951). *The family: A dynamic interpretation.* New York: The Dryden Press.

Watzlawick, P., Beavin, J., & Jackson, D. D. (1967). *Pragmatics of human communication.* New York: W. W. Norton.

Watzlawick, P., Weakland, J. H., & Fisch, R. (1974). *Change: Principles of problem formation and problem resolution.* New York: W. W. Norton.

Weeks, G. R., & Gambescia, N. (2002). *Hypoactive sexual desire: Integrating sex and couple therapy.* New York: W. W. Norton.

Weeks, G. R., & L'Abate, L. (1982). *Paradoxical psychotherapy: Theory and practice with individuals, couples, and families.* New York: Brunner/Mazel.

Wynne, L. C., Ryckoff, I. M., Day, J., & Hirsch, S. I. (1958). Pseudo-mutuality in the family relations of schizophrenics. *Psychiatry, 21*, 205–220.

Index